Battleground Europe

Walking Verdun

GW0771480

Battleground series:

With the continued expansion of the Battleground Series a **Battleground Series Club** has been formed to benefit the reader. The purpose of the Club is to keep members informed of new titles and to offer many other reader-benefits. Membership is free and by registering an interest you can help us predict print runs and thus assist us in maintaining the quality and prices at their present levels.

Please call the office on 01226 734555, or send your name and address along with a request for more information to:

Battleground Series Club Pen & Sword Books Ltd,
47 Church Street, Barnsley, South Yorkshire S70 2AS

Battleground Europe

Walking Verdun

Christina Holstein

Christina Holstein

First World War Series Editor

Nigel Cave

Pen & Sword
MILITARY

First published in Great Britain in 2009 by
Pen & Sword Military an imprint of
Pen & Sword Books Ltd
47 Church Street
Barnsley
South Yorkshire
S70 2AS
Copyright © Christina Holstein
ISBN 9781844158676

Typeset in Times New Roman PS 10pt by
Pen & Sword Books Ltd
Printed and bound in the United Kingdom by
CPI UK

Pen & Sword Books Ltd incorporates the Imprints of Pen & Sword
Aviation, Pen & Sword Maritime, Pen & Sword Military, Wharncliffe
Local History, Pen and Sword Select, Pen and Sword Military
Classics and Leo Cooper.
For a complete list of Pen & Sword titles please contact
PEN & SWORD BOOKS LIMITED
47 Church Street, Barnsley, South Yorkshire, S70 2AS, England
E-mail: enquiries@pen-and-sword.co.uk
Website: www.pen-and-sword.co.uk

Contents

Introduction by Series Editor

This is a book that all visitors to the battlefields of Verdun 1916 will welcome. All of us who have been to this evocative, menacing, impressive – almost overwhelmingly so – place will be grateful to have the clear and lucid guide that has been so well crafted by Christina Holstein.

We have had quite some time to wait for this; it was in 2002 that Christina's outstanding *Fort Douaumont* in this series was published. But the passing time has not been wasted and the results of her labours and considerable knowledge of both events and ground are now available to all of us.

Verdun really has needed a book like this: there are plenty of guides to notable positions on the Verdun battlefield – such as Forts Douaumont and Vaux, but nothing of any great consequence beyond that. There are excellent narrative histories of the battle, not least Alistair Horne's *The Price of Glory*, and there is a paper mountain of published and unpublished memoirs, diaries and letters. However, because of the sheer slogging match that characterized so much of the fighting; because of the utter confusion of the infantry battles and the almost ceaseless blasting of the landscape (helping to remove 10 metres from one of the summits of Mort-Homme, for example), it is not a battle that lends itself easily to detailed unit accounts, for the most part.

The 'fog of battle' is not the only thing that has made it difficult to understand Verdun. The policy of leaving villages as they were at the end of the war means that there are few landmarks and buildings that help to orientate the visitor. Of greater impact has been the post-war forestation programme, which removes sight lines and minimizes the ability to understand the significance of ground and features. Quite frankly, it is not a battlefield that is easy to understand on the ground; its impact comes from the awesome ossuary and from the hulking concrete ruins that witnessed so much carnage, along with the searing memory it left in the collective consciences of France and Germany.

This book does not clear away the trees and the undergrowth, but it puts you on the trail of the events; it takes you to the crucially important valleys and ravines that formed a vital part in the tactics of both sides; it explains the significance of ruined, decrepit bunkers and fortified systems, hidden away in the forest. It takes you to panoramic views that explain the *raison d'être* of particular fortifications and the significance of topographical features. It puts you on several *via sacra*

A forgotten German cemetery on the edge of the battlefield.
Author's collection.

of the fighting soldiers of France and Germany, men whose courage, fortitude and persistence in the face of such horrendous adversity must surely leave anyone who knows about them filled with awe and horror. Undoubtedly it will provide greater understanding of the story of this, the longest battle of the Great War.

Nigel Cave
Collegio Rosmini, Stresa

Introduction

This is a book about ground. It is not so much a story of what men did but rather of why the particular configuration of the ground forced them to do it that way. It is a book about ridges and ravines where almost nobody walks, the home of wild boar and deer, forgotten and silent, a time warp of early twentieth-century thought and action. Here, the gigantic battle remains in the cratered landscape, the twisted trees, the smashed concrete, the silent trenches and here, with a little imagination, the men still pass.

Verdun has always been all about ground. First, it stands at the crossing point of two traditional communication routes – the River Meuse and the ancient road from Paris to Eastern France and beyond. Second, it is surrounded by hills. On the western side the winding course of the Meuse has cut into both sides of the river valley, leaving

Aerial view of the Verdun Citadel. *H P von Müller's estate*

interlocking spurs that dominate passage along the valley and protect the river crossings. On the eastern side – facing the German border – the hills form high cliffs that drop steeply to a marshy plain. Over the course of time streams have sliced the hills into steep-sided ravines that concentrate communication routes into a few natural gateways and offer scores of natural positions for defence and observation. And what observation! From the top of Fort Douaumont, the highest point in the area, a visitor can look far out over the pre-1914 German border. On a particularly clear day – the sort that comes with the type of east wind that troops must have dreaded – he may even be able to make out the village of St. Privat, forty kilometres away on the north-eastern skyline. Today just a quiet scattering of houses on the outskirts of Metz, St. Privat was the site of an 1870 battle at which the Prussian Guard – attacking uphill against well-sited machine guns forty-six years before the Battle of Verdun – suffered appalling casualties.

Verdun has been fortified since Roman times and Fort Douaumont

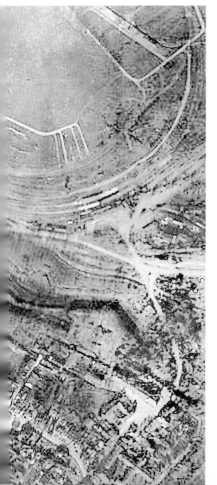

is only one of the works that surround the city. It forms part of the most recent defensive system, which was designed after the defeat of France in the Franco-Prussian War of 1870. Under the peace treaty which brought that war to an end, Germany annexed Alsace and a large part of Lorraine. That brought the German border very close to Verdun, which suddenly found itself in the first line of defence against a future invasion from the east. With only seventeenth-century walls to protect it from the growing power of guns and explosives, a massive fortification programme was implemented. This continued for thirty years until, when the First World War broke out, Verdun was surrounded by a double ring of twenty-eight modern, mutually supporting, armoured forts and fieldworks and a vast number of secondary installations that in-

9

cluded shelters, ammunition depots, observation posts, batteries, narrow gauge railways and strategic roads. It was a position of overwhelming strength. With a garrison of 66,000 men and rations for six months, Verdun was by far the strongest fortress city in France, and in September 1914 the Germans tried to pinch it out rather than face the guns. The attempt was unsuccessful and at the end of the First Battle of the Marne the Germans retired to new lines, leaving Verdun intact but with its main supply lines damaged or destroyed. As a result, throughout 1915 the city was dependent for reliable supply on a single light railway and one road.

Verdun's resources did not remain intact for long. During 1915 the urgent demands for men and materials on other parts of the French front, coupled with the belief – resulting from the speedy fall of the Belgian fortresses in 1914 – that fixed fortification no longer had any role to play in modern warfare, led the French Commander-in-Chief, General Joffre, to disarm the mighty fortress city. Astonishing as it may seem today, by the end of the second year of the war Verdun had been stripped of men, guns, ammunition and supplies.

This was the place that General Erich von Falkenhayn, the Chief of the German General Staff, chose as the target for an offensive that would bring the war to an end in 1916. He believed France to be on the point of military and economic exhaustion and that a further major offensive would persuade her that the war could not be won. With France out of the war, there would be no reason for Britain to go on fighting and Germany would be victorious. Victory had so far eluded the Germans. They had gone to war in August 1914 with a plan that involved swiftly defeating France before turning on Russia and achieving quick victory there. It failed, and as stalemate developed the German High Command was forced to accept the idea that the only way to achieve victory was by wearing the enemy down. For Falkenhayn this concept – which was known as attrition – involved finding an objective that the French High Command would feel obliged to defend at all costs. Verdun was such an objective. Formerly the most important fortress city in France, it was now dangerously situated in a salient divided by a river, stripped of resources and difficult to supply. But there would be no supply difficulties for the Germans. Within fifty kilometres of

General Erich von Falkenhayn, the Chief of the German General Staff.
H P von Müller's estate

Verdun there were huge mineral reserves, steel mills and factories working at full capacity and a massive rail network. In addition, the extensive forests to the north of the German lines offered shelter and camouflage for men, supplies, camps and workshops – everything, in fact, that they needed to supply a major offensive.

In December 1915, General von Falkenhayn submitted to Kaiser William II, the head of the German armed forces, a proposal for a major operation to be launched at Verdun the following February. The Kaiser accepted the proposal, which involved an assault by three army corps on the Right (east) Bank of the River Meuse. No provision was made for reserves. Crown Prince William of Germany, the Commander-in-Chief of the Fifth Army, whose troops were to be used, protested that such an assault would leave the units advancing on the Right Bank at the mercy of the French guns on the opposite side of the

Kaiser William II, head of the German armed forces.
Author's collection.

river. He was ignored. As time was short, infantry units were pressed into service as construction workers, ignoring officers' protests that the work was destroying their attacking spirit. On 12 February 1916 – the date originally chosen for the start of the offensive – the assault troops were in position, but bad weather forced the operation to be postponed. It was 21 February before the German guns finally roared into action, signalling the start of the longest battle on the Western Front.

The fighting raged for three hundred days and nights. At first the French fell back, but the line stiffened once General Pétain took over and new troops were poured in. The Crown Prince's fears proved correct and within two weeks the offensive had been extended to the Left Bank, where the fighting for the Mort-Homme and Hill 304 reached new heights of ferocity. Desperately hurling men into the battle and racing to

Crown Prince William of Germany, the Commander-in-Chief of the Fifth Army.
H P von Müller's estate

11

construct new supply lines, the French hung on. With the hills offering the French all-round observation and fire and an interlocking defensive system covering the valleys, all the Germans could do was slog their way forward, fighting for the high points no matter what the cost, gradually pushing onwards but always visible from the next high ground. It was, quite literally, uphill work. As the months went by the Germans succeeded in capturing two of the most important French forts but failed to reach a position from which they could impose terms. Finally on 11 July, five months into the battle and stretched to the utmost at Verdun, the Somme and the Eastern Front, General von Falkenhayn ordered the Fifth Army to go on the defensive. But the French kept on attacking and by the end of the year the forts and much of the lost ground were in French hands once more.

From the start, Verdun was a battle of superlatives; more guns, more shells, more men, more casualties than ever before. For the Germans, it was all in vain. They did not reach Verdun and the French did not surrender. Launched to bring France to its knees, the Battle of Verdun became a furnace which sucked in French and Germans alike – over 700,000 men killed, wounded and missing, many of whom still lie where they fell. From Hill 304 and the Mort-Homme to Douaumont, Vaux and Fleury – places whose names are repeated on streets, squares and monuments across France and Germany – the pleasant landscape of fields and forests was reduced to a vision of hell, a lunar landscape of horror, filth, fear and confusion.

Seeing the utter destruction of the battlefield, the French government decided that no one should ever live there again. The nine villages swept away by the battle were not rebuilt, and returning refugees were turned away. The forestry department took over and, as the years went by, trees covered the shattered landscape. But the scars remain and from the beech-clad slopes of Colonel Driant's front line to the spectacular cratering around Fort Douaumont and the utter destruction of Fleury, the ground tells the story of the apocalyptic events that were life and death to so many men.

A visitor who seeks to understand what happened here will find in these silent woods and empty valleys a living echo of those days. He will also find a continuing memory of the awesome courage and endurance of the men who fought the Battle of Verdun, 'ordinary' men, both French and German, of whom so much was demanded and whose sacrifice defies belief, imagination or description.

Looking into Porte Neuve, Verdun. *Taylor Library*

Advice to Tourers

The walks: The walks in this book follow as closely as possible the high points of the Battle of Verdun from its start in February 1916 to the French counter-offensive of October 1916. If read or walked in sequence, they will provide a general introduction to the 300-day battle. Each chapter is divided into two parts: an account of the events and a detailed description of the route, together with a simple map. Nos. 1–7 are forest walks, but 8–10 follow roads. For administrative purposes the forest is divided into numbered sections and for ease of navigation block numbers have been included in the route descriptions wherever possible. A 'walking man' sign indicates the start of each walk.

Brief tours of Forts Douaumont and Vaux are included in Nos. 2 and 4, and visits to the Verdun Memorial museum at Fleury may conveniently be added to Nos. 6 and 7.

Ruined houses along the River Meuse, 1916. *Tom Gudmestad*

Getting to Verdun: Verdun lies roughly 450 kilometres south-east of Calais and can easily be reached by car via the A26 and the A4. There are also two possible train services into the city: the three-hour journey via Chalons-en-Champagne or the fifty-nine-minute high-speed (TGV) service, both of which leave from the Gare de l'Est, Paris. The high-speed train stops at the new Meuse TGV station, which is twenty-two kilometres south of Verdun and is connected to the city centre by shuttle bus. At the time of writing there are plans for a summer tourist bus between the city and the main battlefield sites but even if it runs it will not be possible to reach the start of Walks 1–4 by public transport, so visitors arriving by train would still need a car or a bicycle. As car hire possibilities in Verdun are very limited, train travellers would do well to consider hiring in one of the larger centres such as Rheims or Metz. To hire a bike, contact either the *Maison de Tourisme*, Place de la Nation, tel. 0033 3 29 86 14 18, verduntourisme@wanadoo.fr, or the new *Office de Tourisme*, 0033 3 29 84 55 55, tourisme@cc-verdun.fr, which is situated just over the road on the *Ave. Général Mangin*.

Accommodation: The city offers accommodation ranging from three-star hotels to camp sites. However, as car parking in the centre of Verdun is both restricted and fairly expensive, an out-of-town hotel may be a more attractive option. For a full list of accommodation, contact either of the tourist offices above or check this site: http://www.verdun-tourisme.com/www-sommaire_hotels-785-UK-FAMILLE.html.

Some Bed & Breakfast possibilities in the area are listed on: http://www.likhom.com/

Maps: For Walks 1–9 there are two possibilities: either the special IGN battlefield map No. 3112 ET named *Forêts de Verdun et du Mort-Homme; Champ de Bataille de Verdun* or IGN Blue Series Nos. 3212 Ouest and 3112 Est. These are available in Verdun at the *Librairie Duchêne* (the bookshop in the main shopping street) and may also be available on the battlefield. Walk No. 10 is covered by a street map produced by Blay-Foldex and named *Verdun: plan de ville*, which is also on sale in the bookshop. For getting around in the general area there are several possibilities: Michelin No. 307 Local (*Meurthe-et-Moselle, Meuse, Moselle*), Michelin Yellow Series No. 241 (*Champagne-Ardennes*) or IGN Green Series 10 and 11. IGN maps may be bought in advance from the *Institut Géographique National* on www.ign.fr.

Clothing/footwear: Verdun can be very wet, so bring a rainproof jacket and a waterproof bag for camera, pencils and notebook. A torch is also useful. Forest paths are always muddy so make sure you have adequate stout, waterproof footwear. The forts are cool and damp, so carry a sweater or jacket even on a hot day. Make sure your tetanus jab is up to date and that you are properly covered for medical insurance. In summer, bring sun cream and plenty of mosquito repellent, including mosquito spray for your room.

Refreshments: There are a number of authorized picnic sites and the *Abri des Pélerins* café/restaurant, which is near the Ossuary, offers sandwiches, meals and drinks throughout the day. The *Abri* is open from February to December but closed on Mondays. When it is closed, the nearest refreshment possibilities are in Verdun or Bras-sur-Meuse, so plan to carry a snack and plenty of water.

Toilet facilities: Toilet facilities on the battlefield are extremely limited. There are toilets in the Memorial museum and the *Abri des Pélerins* but they are only accessible to clients during opening hours. There are no toilets in the forts, and at the time of writing those behind the Ossuary are also closed.

When to travel: Summer is likely to bring the best weather but the thick forest and dense undergrowth make it difficult to get a feel for the terrain, and the mosquitoes are a nuisance. Autumn and early spring are better, particularly the latter, when the organized hunting season is over. As hunts can temporarily block access to large areas, including the main historical sites, it is a good idea to have an alternative walk in mind. **Please note that the firing range to the north of Fort Douaumont is in use on Mondays and Tuesdays between 8am and midnight. As this restricts access to the Douaumont sector, Walks Nos. 2 and 8 cannot be walked on those days.**

A note on time: During the Battle of Verdun, German time was normally one hour ahead of French time. Any specific time mentioned in this book is French time.

Warning: Most of the battlefield of Verdun is national forest and, while walking is encouraged, visitors should stick to the paths and trails and stay away from the edges of holes. **Collecting 'souvenirs', digging or using metal detectors are absolutely prohibited and subject to heavy fines.** Forts, shelters, dugouts and other positions are dangerous and should not be entered. Live ammunition, shells,

List of Maps and Plans

grenades and mortar bombs should not be touched under any circumstances.

Separate sections at the end of this book contain information on guidebooks, other places of interest in the area and useful addresses.

Memorial to a previous conflict – the Franco-Prussian War and the siege of Verdun 1870-1873. The memorial disappeared during the Second World War. *Taylor Library*

French railway gun.
Taylor Library

Moving up at Verdun.
Taylor Library

An abandoned gun limber, a relic of the battle.
Author's collection

Walk No. 1
THE START OF THE GERMAN OFFENSIVE
21–22 February 1916

Duration: four hours.
Distance: roughly seven kilometres.

This walk covers the assault by the German 21st and 25th Infantry Divisions on the lines held by the French 56th and 59th Battalions of Chasseurs in the Bois des Caures area. It is covered by IGN map 3112 ET and Blue Series 3212 Ouest. There are three short steep sections but the rest is level or downhill. It is likely to be muddy throughout the year. There is a picnic site by the car park opposite the monument to Colonel Driant.

Warning: With the exception of Colonel Driant's command post, any dugouts or concrete positions to be seen on this walk are dangerous and should not be entered. Walkers should stick to the paths and stay away from trenches and the edges of holes.

The events
Of all the positions held by the French on the Right Bank of the River Meuse before the Battle of Verdun began, few were more important than the long wooded hilltop in the centre of the French line approximately twelve kilometres to the north of Verdun. This hilltop was important because it controlled two roads which ran between German lines and the Meuse valley, offering access to Verdun. Since September 1914 the position had been held by the 56th and 59th Chasseurs, two battalions of light infantry reservists whose main priority – apart from holding off the Germans – was to keep warm. To this end they wrapped themselves in anything from blankets to tablecloths, wound enormous mufflers around head and neck, hung their packs with all manner of strange but useful objects and, excellent troops that they were, stood ready at all times with rifles oiled, muzzles plugged and breeches covered to meet whatever attack should come.

Lieutenant Colonel Emile Driant.

H P von Müller's estate

The Chasseurs were proudly commanded by a former career soldier and celebrated public figure, Lieutenant Colonel Emile Driant. A man of outspoken

19

views when it came to the defence of France, Driant had left the army in 1905 to pursue a career as a journalist and author. His literary output – exciting adventure stories involving the scientific and technological developments of his day and drawing a clear distinction between Good and Evil – had made him very popular and in 1910 Driant entered parliament where he worked hard to strengthen national defence. Aged 60 when war broke out, Driant immediately applied for a command even though his age and his parliamentary seat would have exempted him. Having commanded Chasseurs in the past, Driant was delighted to find himself with them again and immediately set about organizing the position near Verdun.

In 1915 a general transfer of men and supplies away from Verdun to more active French sectors dangerously limited the means available. However, the Chasseurs went to work with a will and by the end of that year their position, which lay almost entirely between the present day D125 and D905, was laid out as a series of centres of resistance stretching back over three defensive lines. Furthest forward was the outpost line, which was intended to meet and break the enemy assault. It comprised a series of small positions linked by shallow trenches. From here, communication trenches ran back a short distance to the support line, a series of interconnected positions that included four substantial fieldworks known as *Grand'gardes*. These housed a platoon or more of men and formed the company command posts for each sector of the front. Clear fields of fire between the support positions were ensured by firebreaks, which were barricaded at the sides to prevent an enemy from crossing from one sector to another. Five hundred metres behind the support line was the 'R line', or final line of resistance, comprising a high wire fence, barricades and five strong redoubts. Of these, the most important was R2, a long concrete bunker that also served as Colonel Driant's command post. The distance from R2 to the outpost line was approximately 800 metres. The distance from the outpost line to the German front line varied from two thousand metres to less than thirty metres.

Driant firmly believed that the Germans would attack in Lorraine and during 1915 he complained to the military hierarchy about the neglect of Verdun's defences. When that was unsuccessful, he used his parliamentary connections to raise the alarm and, to the fury of the French Commander-in-Chief, General Joffre, a parliamentary commission was sent to make a report. The commission noted serious deficiencies and in January 1916 some small improvements were made, but limited manpower and heavy rain prevented much from

Colonel Driant's command post. *Author's collection*

being done. However, the weather had one good effect as far as the French were concerned: it led to the postponement of the German offensive, originally planned for 12 February. The German assault troops were already in position when the postponement order was received. At first they remained where they were, but as trenches and dugouts filled with water they returned to camp. It was 20 February before they moved up again, heavily laden with everything from hand grenades and rifles to scaling ladders and infantry shields.

General Joffre.
H P von Müller's estate

The German operation was to take place over two days. On the first day, following an unprecedented artillery barrage along the whole front, small groups of infantry would move forward and occupy the French forward positions while strong patrols of infantry and pioneers reconnoitered ahead to find weak spots. The main assault was to take place on the second day following a further annihilating bombardment.

At 7.12am on 21 February 1916 a massive collection of German guns began to pound the French support lines, batteries and observation posts on the

Right Bank of the Meuse. As the hours went by, gas filled the ravines. Forts and communications came under fire and shells fell in the centre of Verdun. With the main railway lines damaged or cut, French gunners were unsure of their ammunition supply and could only respond weakly. At noon, over 150 trench mortars joined in the fray, bringing the French front lines under fire. The pounding continued until 4pm, when the bombardment lifted and a line of infantry moved out of the German trenches, followed by the patrols. They were armed with rifles, hand grenades and entrenching tools and they did not expect to meet any resistance.

But, to their surprise, there was resistance. The roaring bombardment had not smashed Driant's lines as expected. When it began, the 59th Chasseurs in position between R2 and the front line had taken shelter where they could and now they prepared to fight. On the German right, where the French outpost line had been partly abandoned, the patrols made good progress. Capturing machine guns and prisoners, they reached the R line but found it largely undamaged and strongly defended. Without help from reinforcements or pioneers, no further progress was possible. The situation was more difficult in the centre and on the left, where the front lines were very close together. Here, the Germans met such desperate resistance that they were scarcely able to advance beyond the outpost line at all. As darkness fell, the little groups of Germans either fell back or remained where they were and waited for morning.

Back at R2, Colonel Driant had no clear idea of the situation. During the day the roaring bombardment had not only cut communications but filled the air with smoke and dust, making observation impossible. Out of touch with both the rear and his own front line, Driant went forward during the evening to see the situation for himself. He found that despite the many casualties morale was still good and that while some parts of the outpost and support lines had fallen, most positions were still in French hands, as was most of the R line. Nevertheless, Driant knew that the situation was critical. During the day the Germans had successfully carried the sector on the Chasseurs' left and were already infiltrating along the ravine on their right, where the D905 runs today. All they could do now, Driant told them, was remain in place and fight. As he returned to R2, two companies of the 56th Battalion, which had come up during the day, spread out through the damaged wood as best they could and prepared to fight.

Before dawn on 22 February the Germans retired to the safety of their own lines and at 7am the roaring bombardment began again. This time it targeted the Chasseurs' front line, wiping out the trenches and crushing any hope of an organized counter-attack. The Germans watched in wonder as the rain of shells ploughed into the ground, throwing up columns of dirt and stones and lifting whole trees into the air. At noon the bombardment lifted and the infantry moved forward, supported by pioneers, flame throwers and machine guns. Rockets desperately asking for French artillery support had no effect and the front lines were quickly overrun. With their ammunition exhausted the Chasseurs fought on with bayonets and grenades but, despite rounding up everyone who was still able to fight, including the cooks, runners and telephone operators, they were slowly pushed back. By mid-afternoon their position was hopeless. The Germans had pushed through the forest on either side of the hilltop, leaving the little group – by now concentrated around R2 – open to attack from the rear. During the late afternoon, the Germans manhandled a 77mm field gun through the wood to a position on the D905 close to R2 and began firing at the command post over open sights. Driant calmly ordered a machine gun to be turned to deal with it but a direct hit put the machine gun out of action before the gunners could begin to fire.

Realizing that they had done all they could, Driant ordered his men to withdraw. Having taken leave of the wounded in the first-aid post, Driant set off across the road. He stopped to offer first aid to a wounded man and, standing up, was hit in the head. His men returned

A substantial German position above Flabas. *Author's collection*

to French lines without him and it was April before Colonel Driant's family received definite news of his death.

Although few of the Chasseurs succeeding in reaching French lines, their determined resistance delayed the German advance and caused them several hundred unexpected casualties. It also set an example of courage and self-sacrifice that was to be repeated on many occasions throughout the ten months of the Battle of Verdun.

The walk

To reach the start of this walk take the D964 from Verdun towards Dun-sur-Meuse and Stenay. At Vacherauville, fork right on the D905 towards Damvillers and Colonel Driant's command post (PC Colonel DRIANT). Pass the monument to Colonel Driant, which stands on a left-hand bend at the top of the hill. At the road fork just beyond the bend take the D125 towards Flabas and Moirey, passing Colonel Driant's command post on the left. The monument and the command post will be visited later in the walk. Continue for nearly one kilometre until the road emerges from the forest and passes through open ground. The field on the right-hand side of the road is a roughly triangular. Pull over by the sign indicating a bend in the road and stop. Face ahead.

You are now between the French and German lines of 21 February 1916. The German lines bordered the wood ahead of you, crossed the road and continued along the edge of the field to your right front. The French forward positions bordered the field to your right rear and faced the German lines. Beyond the far end of the field (close to the peak of the triangle), the two lines ran roughly parallel through the forest for approximately 750 metres and in places were less than thirty metres apart.

Continue downhill through the woods towards Flabas and park on the left-hand side of the road at the bottom of the hill just before you reach the first house. Walk back uphill for a few metres and turn left into the wood on the track beginning opposite the 'jumping deer' road sign (**A**). The entrance to the path is indicated by a small red and white card marked 29. Walk uphill for approximately three hundred metres and stop when you reach forest blocks 29 and 33 on the left and 30 and 31 on the right. Face uphill (**B**).

The Germans had been established on this hillside since the end of the First Battle of the Marne in September 1914. At first their positions here were quite simple but, during 1915, infantry and pioneer units laboured to extend them until, by the end of that year, they formed a series of connected strongpoints that included such features as wire,

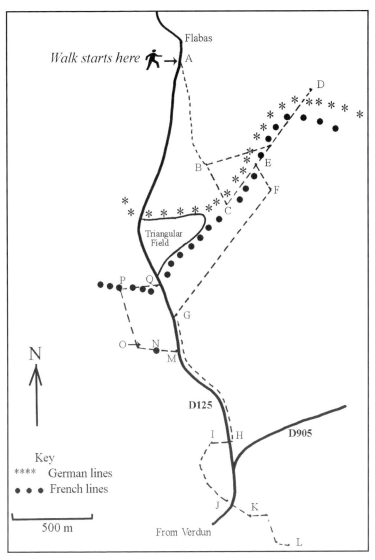

Flabas

Walk starts here A

D

B E

F

C

Triangular
Field

P Q

G

O N
M

D125

I H D905

Key
**** German lines
• • • French lines

N

500 m

J K

From Verdun L

shell-proof dugouts, observation posts, machine gun emplacements and even a heavy trench mortar position. At the beginning of 1916 further development took place when – level with your current position – German pioneers prepared underground troop shelters in preparation for the coming operation. These shelters, known as Stollen, ran in two lines across the hillside some 250 metres behind and parallel with the front line.

German front-line trench and small-arms position. *Author's collection.*

The track to your left between blocks 29 and 33 follows the lower line of Stollen along the hillside for several hundred metres. They appear today as a series of collapsed dugout entrances linked by a trench and connected to the front line by deep communication trenches. I suggest walking along this path as far as block 21 to see the extent and nature of the remaining positions before returning to (**B**) and turning uphill. Continue over the crest of the hill, noting, on the left just beyond the crest, a deep excavation of roughly rectangular shape. With 'fossilized' barrels of cement lying by the edge of the hole, this site was perhaps intended for a blockhouse. Note that the ground shows little shell damage in this area. The trench system clearly visible on both sides of the track is deep and complex and includes a number of damaged observation posts and small arms positions. On 21 February 1916 this track, which existed in 1916, formed the German divisional boundary between the 21st Division (81st and 87th Infantry) on the right and the 25th Division (115th Infantry) on the left.

Continue downhill to the nearby junction in the tracks, turn left and stop (**C**). The track now ahead of you ran between the French and German front lines of 21 February 1916, with the German trenches to the left of the track and the French outpost line to the right. Approximately one hundred metres from where you are standing the outpost line crossed the track from right to left, which brought it very close to the German forward positions. These are extremely well preserved and include a number of small blockhouses, some of which may date from the development of a fortified line named the *Volkerstellung* in 1917–18.

Walk along the track to **(D)**, which will take you past a very impressive trench system, then return to **(E)**. Turn left downhill with block 9 on your left and 8 on your right. This will take you through some of the French support positions, a good example of which is to be seen on the left a short distance downhill. The ground here shows only light shelling. At the next crossroads in the tracks **(F)**, turn right and walk on for about 500 metres (first level, then uphill). Roughly speaking, this path runs between the French support positions on the right and the more substantial *Grand'gardes* on the left. The clearest of these – a sizeable fieldwork partly surrounded by a shallow ditch – is to be seen on the left near the top of the hill at the 13/12 forest block junction.

Observing the the enemy. *Taylor Library*

From this fieldwork, continue to the D125 **(G)** and turn left. Walk along the road for approximately 700 metres, being careful to keep to the grass verge. The substantial concrete position

Observation and small arms position close to R2. *Author's collection.*

that stands by the roadside within sight of the junction with the D905 may have been built by the Germans or they may have merely improved an existing structure. The Chasseurs had a machine gun post here but it is not clear whether it was of concrete.

At the sign for *Retranchement R2 (PC du Colonel Driant), 50 mètres* **(H)**, turn right into the wood and follow the path to the command post **(I)**, which is surrounded by decorative posts added after the war. There is more evidence of shelling in the ground here but R2 was not extensively damaged in the bombardment of February 1916. Follow the gravelled path past the front of the command post and then along a former communication trench (*Boyau de Communication*) to the monument under which Colonel Driant is buried **(J)**. Thirteen unknown Chasseurs surround the grave, which is the focus of a

commemoration ceremony held every February. From there, cross the road and enter the wood, following the sign for *Sentier du Bois des Caures, Stèle du Col. Driant 130 m.* The small stone monument in the clearing ahead marks the site where Colonel Driant was killed **(K)**. To reach his wartime grave continue past the monument to the signs for *Tombe provisoire du Colonel Driant* **(L)**.

The first definite news of Driant's death was obtained by the King of Spain, who was a family friend. Later, the Red Cross informed the French authorities that he had been buried by the Germans alongside the commander of the 59th Chasseurs,

Colonel Driant's grave.
Author's collection.

Commandant Renouard. Following the German withdrawal from the area in October 1918 a French reconnaissance party formally located the graves but it was not until the following year that the bodies were identified. Colonel Driant's coffin was then reburied until, on 21 October 1922, he was finally laid to rest under the monument by the roadside.

Now retrace your steps to the D125. Cross over to the monument and go back towards R2 via the gravel path nearest the road, passing the Chasseurs' first-aid post (*Poste de secours*). Return to the D125, turn left and begin to walk back towards Flabas.

Visitors who do not wish to prolong the walk may now continue directly to Flabas along the D125. Those who wish to see more of Colonel Driant's positions should proceed as follows, bearing in mind that this part of the walk may be very muddy. Continue along the road towards Flabas for approximately 500 metres and turn left by the sign reading *Fôret Domaniale de Verdun* with block 75 on your left and block 4 on your right **(M)**. The wide dirt road may be closed by a wooden barrier but this need not deter walkers. The earthworks to be

The site where Colonel Driant was buried by the Germans. After the war, the original grave marker was replaced by the cross seen in the photograph. It has recently been replaced by a modern headstone.
Author's collection

German infantry shelter and fighting position, 1917–18.
Author's collection

The 8mm St Etienne Heavy Machine Gun in operation. *Taylor Library*

seen on the right as you walk along are all that remains of *Grand'garde 4* **(N)**, which was connected to the former French front line by a deep trench.

Continue to the next junction of tracks and turn sharp right with block 4 on your right and block 55 on your left. On the right, close to the turn, is a fine example of a German strongpoint **(O)**. This post, one of numerous concrete defences built in 1917 and 1918, features a name – *Habicht* (hawk) – over the entrances. The Chasseurs had a machine gun position here before the Battle of Verdun began.

Follow the track to the top of the hill and turn right at the open field **(P)**. Carefully avoiding any crops, follow the edge of the wood downhill, passing a small concrete observation post so placed as to provide an extensive view over German lines along the edge of the wood opposite. This will be difficult to see in summer when the undergrowth is thick. Close behind it is a long concrete shelter from which trenches run back to *Grand'garde 4*. The Chasseurs had a number of machine guns here and the clear field of fire that the position provides is very striking.

Continue downhill to the road **(Q)** and turn left to return to your car.

Walk No. 2

THE GERMAN CAPTURE OF FORT DOUAUMONT

25 February 1916

Duration: four and a half hours, including a tour of Fort Douaumont. *Distance*: nine kilometres.

This walk covers the German assault on Fort Douaumont by units of the 6th Division, which formed part of III Army Corps commanded by General von Lochow. It is covered by IGN maps 3112 ET and Blue Series 3212 Ouest.

There is a steep stretch between Hassoule Ravine and Fort Douaumont but otherwise the route is either level or downhill. It is likely to be muddy throughout the year. There is a picnic site by the chapel in Bezonvaux. Bring a sweater or jacket for the visit to the fort.

Note: The direction taken by the German assault on Fort Douaumont crosses the modern firing range and is normally inaccessible. This walk therefore follows a supply route used by thousands of German troops going into the Douaumont sector. **It cannot be walked on Mondays and Tuesdays, when the firing range is in operation.**

The events

In 1914 the most important feature of the vast defensive system surrounding Verdun was Fort Douaumont, a huge, sunken, concrete-covered construction situated at the highest point on the Right Bank of the River Meuse, from where the views stretched for miles in all directions. Its reputation as the most powerful fort in the sector was well known to the advancing Germans. They looked at it with trepidation, fearing that the concrete carapace would resist the most powerful shells and that its capture would cost them dear.

The fort that faced the Germans in 1916 bore little resemblance to the original 1880s construction. Thirty years of continuous development aimed at protecting it from the increasing power of guns and explosives had transformed a traditional stone-built work into a modern, armoured fort of enormous strength, whose low profile was specifically designed to deflect artillery. This had been achieved by banking earth up around the lower floor of the fort's main block and

31

Aerial view of Fort Douaumont in 1915. *H P von Müller's estate*

covering the upper floor – which was now at ground level – with a massive layer of concrete. This was laid on a buffer of sand and further protected by a deep layer of earth. The guns, which originally stood on the parapet, were at first dispersed into external batteries and then housed in shell-proof positions inside the fort, which were linked to the main block by strong underground tunnels. Surrounding the whole construction was a deep ditch protected by armoured concrete bunkers and, outside the ditch, a wide field of wire.

Although it was the cornerstone of French defence in the area, Fort Douaumont came to be regarded as a white elephant once the war began. When forts in Belgium and on the Eastern Front proved unable to resist the German advance, the French High Command decided that fixed fortifications no longer served any useful purpose. As a result, Fort Douaumont was stripped of its movable armament and supplies and left in the care of an elderly warrant officer and a small group of territorials.

For the first few days of the battle, the German advance was rapid and by the evening of 24 February the leading units were little more than two kilometres from the fort. At 3pm the following day the bombardment lifted and they jumped off, with orders to stop some 800 metres short of the fort. They rushed the nearest French positions, capturing guns and scattering the French. Many were taken prisoner while others fled, leaving the slopes in front of the fort empty of defenders. Surprised by their success, the attackers – units of the 24th Brandenburg Infantry Regiment accompanied by pioneers – set off in happy pursuit but ran into machine gun fire from a nearby church tower. Scattering for cover into a long defile named Strawberry Ravine, they moved towards the fort, which they could now see clearly. One of the turret guns was firing but there were no defenders on the glacis and the prisoners taken earlier had said that the fort was only weakly held. Had the assault troops but known it, since the start of the battle the little garrison had been taking cover on the lower floor of the barracks. The observation posts were unoccupied and the only gun firing was aiming at targets that had been fixed since the early months of the war.

The Brandenburgers had already gone beyond their objective and now they hesitated. As they did so, the German bombardment started again, softening up the fort for the following day's assault. In the circumstances, it was as dangerous to stay where they were as to go on and, independently of one another, two officers of the 24th – Lieutenant Eugen Radtke and Captain Hans Joachim Haupt – decided to head towards the fort. Haupt fired off flares, vainly hoping that German observers would see them and lift the barrage but by now snow was falling and in the fading light the flares were not seen. Ahead of the Brandenburgers, a trench that ran around the fort seemed to offer better cover than the open ground where they now stood, and they began to cut a way through the wire to reach it.

As they did so, the machine gun fire from the church died away. The defenders of Douaumont village had seen the flares rising into the air and wondered at the lack of response from the fort. Now as they peered into the gloom they saw, just a couple of hundred metres away, what appeared to be small groups of men moving towards the fort, well ahead of where the Germans had last been seen. Incredulously, they watched them march into their own barrage and for a few minutes held their fire, believing them to

Lieutenant Eugen Radtke, the first German officer into the ditch of Fort Douaumont.
H P von Müller's estate

be retreating Zouaves – French colonial infantry – sent up that morning to reinforce the area in front of the fort. By the time they changed their minds the first Germans had safely reached the top of the ditch. Here they met a fresh obstacle – a high iron railing. Spreading out along it they soon found a breach blasted by a shell that had left a pile of rubble at the bottom of the ditch. In the absence of ropes or ladders, one of the sergeants knotted his rifle sling to Radtke's and, holding on to the railing and leaning down as far as he could, he helped Radtke to slide down into the ditch. He then slithered down himself and others followed.

It was now 4pm. The Germans had reached the ditch but to be safe they had to get into the barracks. The door into the nearby bunker was bolted so, with their own shells falling around them, they began to crawl up the steep slope to the top of the fort. Reaching the top, Haupt and Radtke got their men into the barracks from the rear. There was no one about and after the noise outside, the silence inside seemed menacing. With rifles and hand grenades at the ready the Germans moved quietly along the main corridor until, from behind a closed

Main gate of Fort Douaumont in January 1916.
Taylor Library

Werner Beumelburg. Aged only 17 when he arrived at Verdun, the young Beumelburg saw epic service with the 30th Pioneers in and around Fort Douaumont throughout the Battle of Verdun. His detailed and deeply moving account of the fighting for Fort Douaumont and of life inside the fort, published in 1925, forms the first volume of *Schlachten des Weltkrieges*, the German narrative history of the war.
By kind permission of the Beumelburg family.

door, they heard voices speaking French. Putting some broken French phrases together, a lieutenant ordered the French soldiers to surrender. There was a silence and before anything else could happen, more Germans arrived, bringing with them a captured French gunner. He led them down to the lower floor of the barracks where the tiny garrison was sheltering.

With the fall of Fort Douaumont, France lost not only the strongest and most modern of

35

its defensive works at Verdun but also the best observatory in the sector. Its commanding position was so important that it had to be retaken if the Right Bank was to be held. The Germans had to hold it if they were to continue their assault. Between 25 February and 24 October 1916 the determination to hold or to retake Fort Douaumont dominated the campaign and drove both sides to the limits of endeavour and endurance.

The walk

This walk begins at the destroyed village of Bezonvaux. To reach the start of the walk take the D603 from Verdun towards Etain (NB: on the IGN maps, this road is still numbered N3). The road crosses the Meuse Heights and drops down to a roundabout close to the village of Eix. At the roundabout turn left on the D24. Drive straight through the village of Damloup and continue to Bezonvaux. Pass the war memorial, which stands on the left by a bend in the road, and turn left by the sign reading *Chapelle de Bezonvaux* and park by the chapel.

Bezonvaux

Before August 1914 Bezonvaux was a peaceful village whose inhabitants earned a living from country crafts, farming and commerce. It became busy with French troops as soon as war broke out and by mid-September most of the inhabitants had left. With the German lines little more than three kilometres to the north, Bezonvaux became the headquarters of an unusual group of men who based themselves in the former café. They had been brought together by André Maginot, a member of parliament and former secretary of state for war who had joined up as a private soldier on the outbreak of war. Camped with his regiment on the heights above Bezonvaux, from where the views stretched for miles over the German positions, Maginot saw an opportunity for interfering with the enemy patrols assigned to explore the region. For three months his 'elite section' patrolled the deserted villages between the lines, lying in wait for Germans units and informing on their movements. The reports proved useful and Maginot was promoted to corporal. In November 1914 a serious injury sustained in a German ambush cut short his military career but by then the exploits of his picked band were famous throughout France.

Bezonvaux fell to the Germans on 26 February 1916 and immediately became a major logistic and supply centre. A dressing station was set up in the old chateau, and field kitchens were

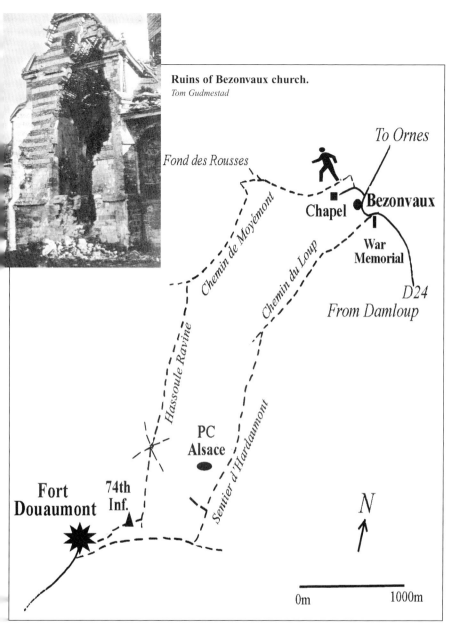

Ruins of Bezonvaux church.
Tom Gudmestad

Fond des Rousses

To Ornes

Chapel

Bezonvaux

Chemin de Moyémont

Chemin du Loup

War Memorial

D24
From Damloup

Hassoule Ravine

PC Alsace

Sentier d'Hardaumont

Fort Douaumont

74th Inf.

N

0m   1000m

established. Traffic jams became frequent as troops and supply services going up to the line ran into those coming out. Recaptured by the French in December 1916, the village remained a target for shelling and by the end of the war it was so devastated that the refugees were not allowed to return. Hidden in dense vegetation for years, the

French prisoners being marched away. *Taylor Library*

site has recently been cleared. White posts among the ruins mark the site of the individual dwellings and bear the names of the families that lived there before life in the old village was swept away for ever.

Chemin des Rousses

To begin the walk, follow the uphill path close to the chapel which leads to an information plinth and the breech of a French 155mm field gun. At the gun, turn right uphill towards the trees. Go up the steps on to the forest road named on the IGN maps *Chemin des Rousses* and turn left. From March 1916 a narrow gauge railway line, part of the extensive German railway system in the area, ran along this track. Two sections of the line, one of them seriously damaged, are now to be seen in the destroyed village at the rear of the chapel.

Continue for approximately one kilometre until you reach a white sign for the firing range (*Zone Dangereuse*) which stands on the right of the track. Stop and look straight ahead.

Fond des Rousses

The valley in front of you – *Fond des Rousses* – was immensely important to the Germans throughout the Battle of Verdun and, as in Bezonvaux, traffic frequently came to a halt here. The left-hand side of the valley not only offered sheltered positions for camps and batteries but allowed secure access to the Douaumont sector through a number of steep-sided ravines. Being well supplied with water, the valley was always crowded with water details, who even came here from Fort Douaumont. The journeys to and from the fort were so dangerous that the water parties were known, with grim humour, as the Ascension detail.

Chemin de Moyémont

Just beyond the firing range sign, turn left on to a grassy path that crosses the valley. Pass the stream and continue uphill to a crossroads in the tracks, then turn left. On map 3112 ET this track is named *Chemin de Moyémont*. Follow the level track around the hillside. Over the next two kilometres, note the many signs of battle on both sides. Pass several firing range signs – including a skull and crossbones on a faded red background – and continue alongside a deep communication trench to a fork in the tracks with forest block 327 on the right and 338 ahead of you. Strawberry Ravine, into which the Germans ran for shelter on 25 February 1916, is directly ahead.

Hassoule Ravine

Take the left-hand fork downhill and cross the valley bottom. At the junction with the track on the opposite hillside, stop and face uphill. You are now in Hassoule Ravine. This was a vital German supply route for the Douaumont sector and as such it was in constant use throughout the battle. At all times an atmospheric place, this ravine is particularly striking in winter when trenches and traces of the battle are clearly visible. Being sheltered from incoming shellfire, the steep hillside on the left was the site of numerous camps, dumps and command posts.

The great explosion

On 8 May 1916 the 2nd Battalion of the 24th Brandenburg Infantry – in reserve in this ravine – awoke to the stunning news that the French had blown up Fort Douaumont. Emerging from their dugouts they were shocked to see men streaming down the ravine with staring eyes, blackened faces and tattered uniforms. They tried to find out what had happened but the men refused to stop. Some were hysterical while others were unable to speak. Desperate for news of the 3rd Battalion, which had gone into the fort the previous day, they finally managed to grab hold of a pioneer lieutenant and manhandle him into the battalion command post, where a doctor administered a large dose of brandy. This brought the lieutenant to his senses but he was still unable to explain what had happened. All he could remember was being woken in the fort by three enormous explosions that blew the doors out and filled the corridors with black smoke. There was screaming and panic as men rushed to get out, trampling the wounded as they did so. Doors became blocked with bodies as men fought with one another in an attempt to reach fresh air.

Realizing that a major incident had taken place, the Germans dispatched medical assistance and breathing apparatus to Fort Douaumont but with the corridors full of smoke and fumes, it was some days before the full casualty list was known. It ran to nearly 2,500 names, almost 700 of whom were dead. To the particular sorrow of the 24th, they included the 3rd Battalion's commander, his adjutant, the commander of the machine gun company and all the runners, signallers and orderlies.

Wishing to bury their comrades in the regimental cemetery, men were sent from this ravine to bring back the bodies but, faced with a 'man high' stack of charred and unidentifiable remains, they realized that it was impossible. Together with the other casualties of that terrible May morning, the dead of the 3rd Battalion were carried through the fort and buried in two of the artillery shelters at the rear of the barracks, where they still lie.

Now proceed uphill until you reach a junction of six tracks and stop. Although it is difficult to imagine today, the constant bombardment had removed all vegetation from this area by the end of April 1916, leaving Fort Douaumont – which is less than one kilometre ahead – clearly visible. Cross over to the path between blocks 355 and 354 and follow it uphill for approximately 500 metres, turning right at the sign marked *Monument du 74ieme RI*. You are now very close to Fort Douaumont and the deep shell craters stretch in all directions.

74th Infantry memorial.
Author's collection

74th Infantry memorial

This memorial stands on the site of a retractable gun turret and observation post that were unfinished when war broke out. It was captured by the Germans on 26 February 1916 and quickly became important, as it provided secure facilities for directing artillery fire over nearby French positions. During the first French attempt to retake Fort Douaumont in May 1916 this ridge was attacked by the 3rd Battalion of the 74th Infantry. They reached it after bloody hand-to-hand fighting but were forced to surrender the following day with casualties of over 70 per cent. This position was finally retaken by the French on 24 October 1916.

From the memorial, continue along the path to the car park of Fort Douaumont, which is a short distance ahead. Recent clearance along the right-hand side of the path leaves no doubt as to the great size and power of the fort.

A brief tour of Fort Douaumont

For a detailed history of the fort and the events surrounding it, see *Fort Douaumont – Verdun* in the Battleground Europe series.

The exterior

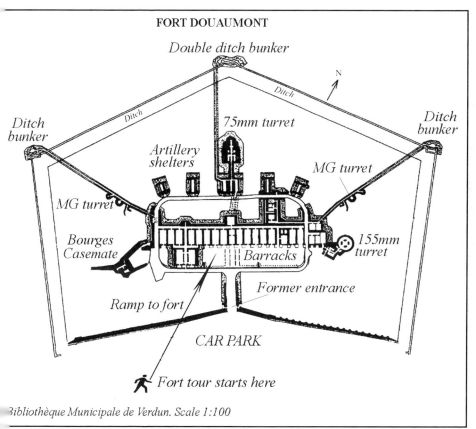

FORT DOUAUMONT

Double ditch bunker

Ditch

N

Ditch bunker

Ditch

75mm turret

Ditch bunker

Artillery shelters

MG turret

MG turret

Bourges Casemate

Barracks

155mm turret

Former entrance

Ramp to fort

CAR PARK

Fort tour starts here

Bibliothèque Municipale de Verdun. Scale 1:100

The car park occupies part of the glacis and ditch on the south side of the fort. The old gateway, to be seen behind the fence when you reach the car park, is all that remains of the blockhouse that originally guarded the main entrance. The tunnel allowed wagon access to the barracks through the earth rampart. The ditch which surrounds the fort is accessible but care should be taken to avoid the picket posts and iron bars that still protrude.

The barracks and superstructure

To tour the outside of the fort, walk up the ramp from the car park. The building ahead of you is the former barracks. Turn right along the façade, passing the visitor entrance. As you do so, note the thick layer of concrete covering the original stone construction and the extensive shell damage. After the war was over it was calculated that the fort had been battered by at least 120,000 shells. Only the French 400mm and German 420mm shells succeeded in piercing the concrete and the lower floor remained habitable throughout the battle. The present appearance of the façade dates from French reconstruction work carried out in 1917–18.

Façade of Fort Douaumont then (January 1916) and now. *Author's collection*

Continue to the blockhouse at the end, which houses the 155mm gun turret. This is the heaviest of the four rotating gun turrets at Fort Douaumont. The massive steel cupola that covers the single-barrelled gun resisted the impact of even the heaviest shells. After the French recaptured the fort they found the turret mechanism to be undamaged and the gun was soon returned to action. The adjacent small steel dome protects the observation post from which artillery fire was controlled and directed. Recent clearance of the ditch has revealed the astonishing extent of the views available from the top of the fort. The nearby small gun turret and observation post housed two Hotchkiss machine guns for the close defence of the fort.

From the 155mm turret, walk to the concrete dome that stands on the highest point of the fort and shelters an observation post built by the French in 1917. From there, continue towards the 75mm gun turret and observation post which are ahead of you and slightly to the left. During the German occupation of the fort this turret was used by the Germans as a signalling station. It is not open to visitors. The damage visible to one of the gun barrels occurred during the Second World War.

Stand with your back to the cupola and face ahead. The bare rectangular area ahead of you is the modern firing range, which roughly covers the German line of advance on 25 February 1916. The largest of the ditch bunkers is visible below. During the first French attempt to retake Fort Douaumont in May 1916, French troops reached this gun turret and occupied the top of the fort between where you are standing and the ditch on your extreme left. However, they failed to gain entrance to the barracks, and the area to your right remained in German hands.

Continue towards the second machine gun turret, which was completely destroyed in the run-up to the French recapture of the fort on 24 October 1916. The present turret was installed during the 1930s. From here, look back towards the highest point. The artillery shelters in which the casualties of the May explosion were buried stood to the left of a line between that point and where you are now. No trace of the shelters can be seen today.

Now follow the path down towards the front of the barracks. The heavily damaged blockhouse to the right of the steps is the Bourges Casemate, a strong concrete bunker that originally housed two 75mm fortress guns. A comparison between this battered ruin and the identical, restored, casemates at Fort Vaux will clearly show the terrible power of the shells that fell here during the battle. To the left of the

Top of Fort Douaumont after the war. *Author's collection.*

steps the original entrance to this end of the barracks has been almost entirely lost in the blockhouses built by the French after they recaptured the fort.

Continue towards the visitor entrance and stop in front of the extension to the barracks. This was added in 1887. The battle totally destroyed the front of the extension and the existing blockhouses were built in 1917–18.

The interior

From the extension, continue to the visitor entrance. Once in the main corridor, turn left. When the fort was built the metal ladders on the right-hand wall of this corridor provided access to the water cisterns on

A barrack room in Fort Douaumont. *Author's collection*

the floor below. Note that the roof here has been repaired. In this area of the fort, the concrete covering on the roof was only one and a half metres thick and it did not resist the heaviest shells. From the first room on the left, which houses a useful relief map, continue towards the walls that block the corridor. The inaccessible corridor on the right just before you reach them leads to the 75mm gun turret and nearby ditch bunker. Once past the walls you are in the redoubt or 'keep' of Fort Douaumont. Here the concrete covering was two and a half metres thick and no shells pierced it. Continue along the corridor and turn left at the sign reading *Merlon Sud* to visit the extension. Before the battle, the fort's commandant and officers had their quarters in this area of the fort. After the battle the French established a forge and workshop in the extension and installed a water cistern and filtration plant.

Return to the main corridor and turn left towards the German cemetery (*Cimetière Allemande*). The doorway at the end of the corridor leads to the western wagon road, one of the two roads that ran through the barracks to the artillery shelters outside.

Turn right when you reach the wagon road. Ahead of you is the memorial to the casualties of the terrible explosion of 8 May 1916, who were carried out through the tunnel for burial outside the barracks. A commemorative plaque on the wall to the left of the memorial records the event. The adjacent corridor leads to the north-western machine gun turret and ditch bunker. Through the narrow gateway now behind you a very dilapidated corridor leads to the Bourges Casemate. During their first – unsuccessful – attempt to retake Fort Douaumont in May 1916, French troops managed to seize the Bourges Casemate and some even penetrated along the corridor far enough to see machine guns installed here. They retreated quietly and held the Bourges Casemate for two days before being forced to surrender.

Now return to the main corridor and take the first left at the sign reading *Etage Inférieure*. Go down to the lower floor, noting the flight of steps on the left which leads to the former German hospital. This is inaccessible and generally flooded.

The lower floor
The rooms along the right-hand side of this corridor were originally water cisterns. During 1915 most of them were drained for use as storerooms and the present corridor access was created. The washing facilities in the second room may not be a 1916 feature. The third room housed electricity generators installed after the battle.

Halfway along the corridor a 30m-deep shaft forms the entrance to a network of deep tunnels dug by the French in 1917–18. These linked the fort's central command post to the ditch bunkers and gun turrets and provided safe access to the fort from several hundred metres away beyond the car park.

The fire that led to the May explosion appears to have started on the far side of this shaft. It spread to the corridor outside the next three cisterns, where a large number of French 155mm shells were still stored along the wall. It is thought that the fire made the shells explode, throwing red-hot metal into a cistern opposite that was used by the pioneers to store hand grenades and detonators. On 23 October 1916 another major fire in this depot led to the partial evacuation of the fort. All three of these cisterns are now inaccessible and the former pioneer depot has been blocked up.

Continue along the corridor to the Powder Magazines (*Magasins à Poudre*), which are on the left of the stairs. During the German occupation of the fort the rear magazine served as the commandant's quarters. Go up the stairs and walk straight along the corridor ahead of you. Cross the eastern wagon road and follow signs to *Tourelle de 155* through a number of small rooms and the latrine block to the 155mm gun turret.

Like the other gun turrets at Fort Douaumont, this one was activated by a vertical movement that raised it into the firing position and lowered it again once the gun had ceased firing. When retracted the gun was hidden from view and entirely protected by the massive steel dome that you saw outside. Although the turret mechanism was extremely advanced, the noise level and the poor ventilation made working conditions very difficult and in practice limited the rate of fire. Throughout the German occupation of the fort, this turret served as a signalling station and troop latrine.

Now return to the barracks, following signs to the exit (*Sortie*) and taking the left-hand corridor when you cross the eastern wagon road. To find the exit, look for the barrel of a 75mm turret gun on the corridor floor. The exit is opposite.

Return to Bezonvaux

After visiting Fort Douaumont return to the car park and head towards the road away from the fort. Just after the end of the car park, turn left on to a wide grassy track signposted *Sentier de Douaumont, Sentier d'Hardaumont*. The Hardaumont track is marked by a red circle on a white ground. Pass the green and white barrier and continue ahead. Before the battle, this track led to the *Ouvrage d'Hardaumont*, one of

Aerial view of Fort Douaumont during the Battle of Verdun.
H P von Müller's estate

Inset: Fort Douaumont during shelling, May 1916.
H P von Müller's estate

a series of fieldworks situated on the edge of the Meuse Heights with commanding views over the German positions. The fieldworks were served by a light railway, which was destroyed during the Battle of Verdun but relaid during 1917. At the same time, a long tunnel was constructed between the railway and Fort Douaumont to allow heavy material and supplies to be brought into the fort on rails.

At the hard road approximately one kilometre further on, turn left between forest blocks 354 and 352 still following the red circles. When you reach the sign for *Emplacement du PC Alsace*, stop. During the Battle of Verdun *PC Alsace* was an important German command post, first-aid post and relay station for stretcher bearers passing from the Douaumont sector to Hassoule Ravine. It was situated in a nearby quarry. After the French recaptured the quarry, a road was laid from here to Bezonvaux to allow the evacuation of wounded by motor ambulances driven by young Americans.

From here, carry on downhill following the sign for *Sentier d'Hardaumont. Itinéraire normale. Mt. de Bezonvaux 2680 m.* You are still following the red circles. Continue for a little over one kilometre to the junction with a wider, sandy road, which on the IGN maps is named the *Chemin du Loup*. Turn right and walk downhill, noting the extensive views over the plain in front of you. The forests that you see ahead provided the Germans with cover for all the facilities needed to supply a major offensive, from camps, gun pits and railways to hospitals and bottled water plants.

Evacuation of wounded by motor ambulance. *Taylor Library*

Walk down to the D24. The substantial war memorial on the right of the road junction commemorates the men of Bezonvaux who fell during the First World War. They include Nicolas Gilles, who was killed in the ambush that brought André Maginot's military career to an end. The bronze plaque on the front shows the main street of Bezonvaux before 1914, while a plaque on the left-hand side lists the men who fell resisting the German advance in June 1940. The small monument on the left of the junction is one of a series erected after the war by the *Touring Club de France*. The inscription reads *Ici fut repoussé l'envahisseur* – 'Here the invader was driven back'. From the junction, turn left towards Bezonvaux to return to your car.

Walk No. 3
THE MORT-HOMME AND HILL 304
March–May 1916

Distance: there are two possible routes: 1. A round trip of approximately five kilometres via Cumières and the Mort-Homme; 2. A short discovery path of 1.3 kilometres.
Duration: approximately two and a half hours for the round trip and forty-five minutes for the discovery path.

This walk is covered by IGN maps 3112 ET or Blue Series 3212 Ouest and 3112 Est. It is likely to be muddy throughout the year.

Warning: When walking the Mort-Homme visitors should stick to the paths and stay away from the edges of holes.

A note on heights: the Mort-Homme has two summits. The French Official History maps show the northern and southern peaks as 286 metres and 295 metres high respectively but constant shelling blasted 10 metres off the southern summit, which is today 285 metres high.

The events
When General Erich von Falkenhayn, the Chief of the German General Staff, drew up his plan for an offensive at Verdun, it did not include an attack on the Left (west) Bank of the Meuse. From the start, this was criticized by senior commanders, who feared that it would allow the French gun batteries established there to be turned to fire on the Germans as they pushed south on the other side of the river. Their fears were soon realized. Falkenhayn's assurances that the German artillery would easily silence the outmoded French guns proved vain and within a few days the French batteries on the Left Bank were exacting a fearful toll on the German units advancing on the Right Bank. Faced with rising casualties, Falkenhayn was forced to admit that if the German offensive was to continue, the guns on the Left Bank had to be silenced.

There were three main ridges on the Left Bank, two of which were the site of numerous forts and fieldworks. However, the most northerly of the three – a long crest with the sinister name of Mort-Homme, or Dead Man – had not been fortified. This was the objective now chosen by the German High Command. Largely bare of trees, the Mort-Homme offered exceptional possibilities for observation and wide fields of fire in all directions. Its capture would eliminate the French field gun batteries behind it and provide the Germans with extensive views to the south and east. It would also allow them to bring their guns forward to deal with the heavy artillery behind the forts on the two ridges further to the south. Once these were eliminated, the advance on the Right Bank could continue.

The French lines on the Left Bank ran to the north of the Mort-Homme and only a few hundred metres from the German positions. Held by the 67th Reserve Division, which formed part of VII Corps commanded by General de Bazelaire, they included a number of fortified villages and were backed by a stream – Forges Brook – which formed a natural barrier to an enemy advance. They were flanked by two further heights – Hill 304 to the west and Goose Hill to the east – from which French troops could fire on any advancing enemy, and they also included two strongly defended areas of woodland.

The plan for the new German offensive involved a two-pronged assault by the Silesian 12th and 22nd Reserve Divisions, which formed part of VI Reserve Corps commanded by General von Gossler. The 12th was to thrust south across Forges Brook while the 22nd crossed the River Meuse and attacked from the east. The aim was to push the French off Goose Hill and clear the adjacent woodland, thus allowing the 12th Division to take the Mort-Homme without the danger of

The ruins of Chattancourt church after the battle. The bare hillside at the top left of the picture is Mort-Homme. *Author's collection*

War memorial in the destroyed village of Cumières at the foot of the Mort-Homme. *Author's collection*

flanking fire from their left. However, the plan did nothing to reduce the danger of flanking fire from Hill 304 on their right, which – owing to a lack of resources – was not included in the operation.

On 5 March a roaring bombardment crashed down on the French positions on the Left Bank, smashing trenches, overturning gun batteries and tearing up wire on the Mort-Homme and Goose Hill. The next morning, in snow and severe frost, the two German divisions moved off along a five-kilometre front. Goose Hill fell quickly but resistance proved stiffer in the woods, which over the next few days were taken, lost and retaken. In a welter of attacks and counter-attacks by day and night, communications broke down and the lines became so intermingled that Germans were seen in French trenches firing by error on their own advancing men. It was not until 10 March that the woods were finally in German hands and the way was clear for the 12th Reserve Division to begin the assault on the Mort-Homme. Although little more than one kilometre ahead, it took a further four days of desperate fighting for the Germans to reach the northern summit of the hill. When they did so, they found that the French still held the higher, southern peak and between the two were 800 metres of open ground in full view of the terrible French artillery.

51

1. Grabbing some sleep in a communication trench.
2. Colonial infantry in the ditch of Fort Douaumont 24 October 1916. *Taylor Library*

3. The heaviest type of German shell fired during the Battle of Verdun. *Author's collection*

French 24cm naval gun installed on the railway line north of Cumières in August 1915. Targetted by German guns at the start of the Battle of Verdun, it was abandoned on 24 February 1916. *Tom Gudmestad*

Part of the post-war visitor entrance to the Gallwitz Tunnel in Caurettes Ravine. *Author's collection*

By now the Mort-Homme was a vision of hell. The constant artillery barrage – which the Germans called the 'iron curtain' – had smashed the woodland and churned the ground into a sea of shell holes in which men fought, slept and died. All trace of vegetation had been blasted away and the original positions were either destroyed or unrecognizable. In the chaos, messengers and reinforcements lost their way, food, water and ammunition failed to arrive and the wounded died before help could arrive. Already the casualty levels were appalling. By 14 March the three assault regiments of the 12th Reserve Division had lost over 3,000 men, while the 67th Reserve Division, which had met the full force of the assault, had to be relieved within three days of the start of the offensive. On both sides battalion after battalion had been reduced to a handful of men and the enormous loss of NCOs and officers – many of whom, from regimental commanders downwards, fell leading their men in the fight for bitterly contested positions – severely affected the fighting value of the units. Casualties were also high among signallers, artillery observers and gunners, with many guns lost and whole batteries withdrawn.

Almost as soon as the operation began it had become clear to the German High Command that it would have to be extended to include Hill 304, from where the French were pouring flanking fire into the German advance. The plan drawn up involved using fresh troops – the elite Bavarian 11th Infantry Division under General von Kneussl – to clear the French from a large area of woodland lying to the west of the hill before taking three villages – Malancourt, Haucourt and Béthincourt – that the French had turned into strongpoints. Unfortunately for the Germans, it also involved bringing huge numbers of men and great quantities of material across Forges Brook, now transformed by shelling into a vast morass that sucked up horses, guns and men. This required superhuman efforts and, with the German preparations clearly visible to the French, daily losses were substantial even before the operation began.

On 20 March a massive German bombardment smashed into the woods west of Hill 304, leaving the French forward positions full of dead and wounded. The demoralized survivors, who included a brigade staff and two regimental staffs, were easily rounded up and a sizeable haul of machine guns and trench mortars passed into German hands. The next step was to clear the villages, from which the French could pour flanking fire into the German advance. But now the French were waiting for them and on 22 March the attack on Malancourt ended in fiasco, with whole battalions slaughtered almost to a man. The attack

54

Monument to the six companies of the French 69th Infantry Regiment wiped out between 30 March and 5 April 1916 while defending Malancourt and Haucourt. *Author's collection*

Trenches captured from the Germans on Mort-Homme August 1917.
Taylor Library

broke down completely and it was with horror in their eyes that the exhausted and mud-covered survivors gradually returned to their starting point. Bringing five fresh divisions into line, the Germans tried again. Malancourt finally fell on 31 March and Haucourt – a mere 500 murderous metres away – on 5 April. On 8 April – with seventeen and a half ammunition trains needed just to get this far – the Germans entered Béthincourt and could at last begin the final assault on Hill 304.

It was accompanied the following day by a full-scale offensive on both banks of the River Meuse. Fighting desperately to hold their positions, men were flung into the apocalypse to fill any breaks in the French line, climbing round smoking craters filled with shapeless debris, broken weapons and corpses. On the Mort-Homme they fought with bayonets and grenades to keep the Germans at bay. Machine gun barrels grew red hot and jammed, telephone wires were cut, messengers disappeared, signals went unseen in the smoke and the wounded died where they lay. But the French line held. Triumphant, General Pétain issued an Order of the Day praising the heroism of all branches of Second Army for breaking the furious German assaults and ending with the stirring words, *Courage! On les aura!*, 'Courage! We'll get them!'

General Pétain, who commanded Second Army at Verdun from 26 February to the end of April 1916. *H P von Müller's estate*

But not yet. For the next month the fighting on Hill 304 see-sawed back and forth. The weather was dreadful. Rain poured down, men drowned in the mud and the difficulties of supplying the front lines became almost insurmountable. Without dry clothes, food or shelter, sickness levels rose alarmingly. On 3 May, the Germans opened fire with over 500 heavy guns, determined that this time they would achieve their objective. For two days the deluge of shells continued, throwing up huge columns of smoke and dust, burying the French troops alive, destroying the dreaded machine guns and preventing the arrival of reinforcements. However, it still took several days of desperate fighting before the Germans finally gained control of the summit and could turn their attention back to the Mort-Homme.

The final German assault on the southern summit of their original objective took place on 20 May. Codenamed 'Ideal', it was prepared with great secrecy and involved five regiments and a massive bombardment of gas and high explosive supported by heavy guns firing from the

Monument to the French 40th Division on the Mort-Homme. *Author's collection*

German troops pass through their own wire on the way to assault French positions. *Taylor Library*

Right Bank. Advancing in successive waves, the assault troops, infantry and carrying parties finally succeeded in reaching their goal. However, they were still taking flanking fire from the village at the foot of the Mort-Homme, and several more days of desperate fighting were needed to clear the ruined houses of French troops and straighten the line.

Although by the end of May the Germans had succeeded in taking both peaks of the Mort-Homme, they had failed to remove the danger to their troops on the Right Bank and had suffered substantial casualties in the process. Moreover, their new lines were on a forward slope and directly in view of the French gunners to the south. Nevertheless, with the operation at an end, the German High Command could turn its full attention back to the Right Bank, where the last desperate attempt to force a decision at Verdun before the start of the Allied summer offensive was preceded by a major German success: the surrender of Fort Vaux.

The walk
To reach the start of these walks, take the D984 from Verdun towards Dun-sur-Meuse and Stenay. At Bras-sur-Meuse, turn left on the D115 towards Charny-sur-Meuse. In Charny, turn right on the D38 following signs to Marre and take either of two routes.

For the discovery path, continue through Marre into Chattancourt.

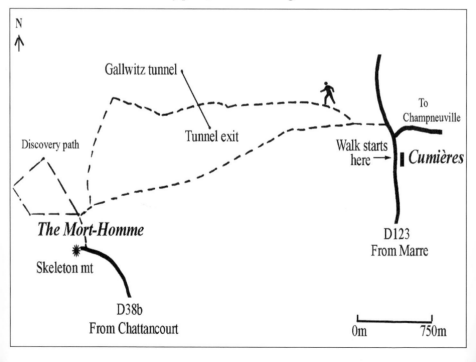

At the Y-fork in the centre of Chattancourt, turn right on the D38b (*Rue de Baley*) following the sign to *Monument de la Crête du Mort-Homme*. Just beyond the last house, note the monument and fountains on the right, which commemorate two victims of the fighting in this area. Drive uphill to the car park and then follow the *Sentier de Découverte* (discovery path) past the wooden barrier. At the nearby crossroads walk straight ahead and after approximately 500 metres turn left into the wood. The path, which is marked by a small blue arrow on a narrow white card, includes a major German trench line (*Silesien Graben*), communication trenches and evidence of heavy shelling. At the end of the walk, return to the car park and walk up to the skeleton monument on the top of the hill. Information about the various monuments on the Mort-Homme is to be found at the end of this chapter.

For the longer walk, drive through Marre towards Chattancourt. Just before Chattancourt, where the D38 makes a sharp bend to the left, continue straight ahead on the D123, following the sign to *Cumières (village détruit)*. Park by the war memorial, which is on the right. The monument on the other side of the road commemorates the Blessed Jeanne Gérard, who was born in Cumières and guillotined in Paris in 1794.

All the images conjured up by the word 'Verdun' are to be found on the Mort-Homme. The endless bombardment, the lunar landscape, the heaps of dead, the unattended wounded, the debris, the stench and the rats were all here on Dead Man's Hill. After the war the area was turned over to forestry but the scars remain and the chaotic landscape, like a frozen sea, still bears witness to the ferocity of the shelling and the unimaginable horror of the battle.

Cumières

The bombardment that blew the top off the Mort-Homme, reducing the height of the southern summit by 10 metres, also destroyed the village of Cumières. Being close to the French front line it was already in ruins when Dr Paul Voivenel, battalion medical officer with the French 211th Infantry and a noted rugby commentator, set up a first-aid post in the cellars of a damaged house. The house soon became a target for German shells, one of which brought down the roof. For a moment it looked as if Voivenel and his men would be buried alive but, when the clouds of dust had settled, they saw light through a narrow gap at ground level. As luck would have it, two fallen timbers were preventing large blocks of masonry from blocking the gap and for the next five hours Voivenel and his men used a pickaxe to dig their way from the cellar to ground level. When everyone was safe, Voivenel, who had narrowly escaped being killed by a shell falling when he was partly out of the gap, set up the first-aid post again in the village chateau. From there, a constant stream of stretcher bearers went to the front lines to bring down the wounded who, after receiving first aid, were evacuated to Marre.

Voivenel and his team were withdrawn on 14 March, by which time the 211th had almost ceased to exist. Of the 2,000 men who had received the full force of the German attack on 6 March, only 200 rifles remained. Two doctors had been killed, the regimental colonel was missing and of the 200, only eighty men were fighting fit.

When recaptured by the 1st March Regiment of the French Foreign Legion in August 1917, Cumières was utterly destroyed. The chateau where Voivenel set up his first-aid post stood behind the church on the far side of the railway. Described by him as a vast building, it is now merely a pile of rubble, hidden by undergrowth during the summer. The only visible traces of the old village are a couple of pre-war graves by the chapel, the old wall at the rear of the cemetery and the mill stream, still flowing from the ruins of the mill by the road to Champneuville.

With your back to the war memorial, turn right along the road. Pass the junction with the road to Champneuville and, immediately after the little bridge, turn left onto a dirt road which is closed by a green and white metal barrier. On the IGN maps this track is named *Sentier de Cumières et du Mort-Homme*. After approximately 250 metres, fork right on to a grassy track with forest block 150 on your left. The track ahead runs into a narrow valley named Caurettes Ravine. In 1916 this ravine was bare of trees apart from one small area of woodland that camouflaged the site of a French naval gun. Running from here to the saddle between the two summits of the Mort-Homme, Caurettes Ravine provided the Germans with shelter and access to the front lines. As you walk along you will see signs of shelling, trenches and collapsed dugout entrances, particularly on the left-hand side. Follow the track uphill to a junction with a wide sandy road, then turn left and walk straight ahead.

The German tunnels
Beginning in the summer of 1916 German pioneers using jackhammers and drills excavated three tunnels in this area with the aim of providing safe access to the front lines and shell-proof

A view inside the Bismarck tunnel. *Markus Klauer*

accommodation for command posts, observation and medical facilities. The shortest of the three was the Bismarck tunnel, which linked the northern and southern peaks of the Mort-Homme. Originally slightly less than 500 metres in length, it was extended northwards in 1917. A longer tunnel named Kronprinz provided access from reserve positions to the German second line, while the Gallwitz tunnel, named after the general in command of the army group on the

Part of the rebuilt entrance to the Gallwitz tunnel. *Markus Klauer*

The Kronprinz Tunnel under Mort-Homme after its capture by the French. *Taylor Library*

German pioneer officers in an underground shelter. *Taylor Library*

Left Bank, allowed troops safe access to Caurettes Ravine from the hillside to your right.

When complete, the Kronprinz and Gallwitz tunnels measured 800–1,000 metres in length, up to three and a half metres in height, and two and a half metres in width. Light rails allowed trucks to bring up building material and remove spoil. Each tunnel had its own garrison, a power plant, telephones, medical facilities and kitchens and provided extensive accommodation for regimental and battalion staffs and for troops. All three tunnels incorporated artillery observation posts and multiple exits equipped with doors that could be closed against gas.

In August 1917, the French launched an offensive aimed at recapturing the Mort-Homme and Hill 304 and pushing the German lines back towards the north. In the shelling, the tunnels became filled with troops, stragglers and wounded, the lights failed and the air became thick and suffocating. In an attempt to clear it, pioneers set up fans at some of the entrances but this merely had the effect of drawing gas into the tunnels so that masks had to be worn. With so many men inside and no possibility of maintaining any sort of sanitation, conditions in the tunnels soon became extremely unpleasant. On 19 August, shells falling at the northern entrance to the Kronprinz tunnel blocked access to the kitchen area. Attempts to dig through the blockage were unsuccessful and only those who managed to climb up a ventilation shaft were able to escape, leaving one hundred men

64

entombed inside. The Bismarck and Kronprinz tunnels were captured on 20 August and their exhausted and gassed garrisons taken prisoner. The garrison of the Gallwitz tunnel held out for a further twenty four hours until, attacked with flamethrowers and without hope of relief, they too surrendered.

The Gallwitz tunnel – incorrectly referred to on the IGN maps as the Kronprinz tunnel – exited at the bottom of the ravine on your left. In recent years these tunnels have been excavated and explored but the entrances are now closed. Visitors wishing to see a similar supply tunnel should consult the Useful Addresses section of this book for details of the Kaiser Tunnel in the Argonne Forest.

Continue for approximately 800 metres until you reach a sign on the left reading *Sentier de Cumières-Mort-Homme, Monument le Mort-Homme 1040m* and turn left. Follow the track uphill over the northern peak of the Mort-Homme, which is now slightly higher than the southern peak. In 1916 this area was completely bare and the Germans who came over the northern hilltop were in full view of the French. Continue to the T-junction with a hard white road and turn right uphill. At the nearby crossroads, turn left. Pass the wooden barrier and take the path by the information boards to the southern summit of the Mort-

Entrance to German underground workings. *Taylor Library*

Homme. The information plinth at the top provides information about the Gallwitz tunnel, while the small monument to be seen on the right when you emerge from the forest gives a brief explanation in French of the German assault.

The monuments

The famous Mort-Homme monument – Death wrapped in a shroud holding an enormous flag and a flaming torch – is dedicated to the officers and men of the French 69th Division who fell in April and May 1916. The inscription reads *Ils n'ont pas passé*, 'They did not pass'. The words are a proud response to General Nivelle's urgent appeal of 23 June 1916, issued when the fall of Verdun seemed imminent: *Vous ne les laisserez pas passer, mes camarades*, 'Comrades, you will not let them pass.'

From here, follow the road down to the car park passing, on the left, a small stone cross dedicated to the German units that fought here in 1916 and a monument to Franco-German friendship. By the monument to the French 40th Division, which fought here between April and June 1916, turn left following the *Sentier de Cumières-Mort-Homme, Cumières 2200m*. Pass the wooden barrier and when you reach the crossroads again, turn right and follow the track downhill to Cumières.

French memorial to the fighting on the Mort-Homme. *Author's collection*

Walk No. 4
THE GERMAN SIEGE AND CAPTURE OF
FORT VAUX
June 1916

Duration: four hours, including a brief tour of Fort Vaux.
Distance: five kilometres.

This walk covers the siege and capture of Fort Vaux by units of the German 50th Infantry Division, which formed part of XV Corps commanded by General von Deimling. It is covered by IGN maps 3112 ET and Blue Series 3212 Ouest.

The first half of the hillside between the mill pond and Fort Vaux is steep but in general the walk is either level or downhill. It is likely to be muddy throughout the year. **Walkers should stick to the paths, stay away from holes in the ground and not attempt to enter either of the infantry shelters described here.** Bring a sweater or jacket for the visit to the fort.

The events

The fall of Fort Douaumont left the German lines on the Right Bank of the Meuse in a dangerously sharp salient and the first French counter-attack was not long in coming. It soon became clear to the Germans that if the fort was to remain in their hands, the lines had to be pushed further away. Unfortunately, the ridge on which Fort Douaumont stood was covered by the guns on a number of other ridges, the nearest of which lay a mere three kilometres to the south. This was the site of three forts – Vaux, Tavannes and Souville – which had been re-armed since the start of the offensive and now formed strong centres of resistance. Any further German advance towards Verdun depended on first removing the dangers presented by this ridge. Of these, the first to be dealt with was Fort Vaux, which commanded all the ground over which the Germans would have to advance.

Vaux was the smallest of the Verdun forts but its commanding position on the eastern edge of the Meuse Heights, from where it overlooked the German positions on the plain below, made it one of the most important. Like the others, it had been overtaken by the revolution in high explosives and artillery that took place during the 1880s. Strengthening its defences involved covering the barracks with a massive coating of concrete and protecting the ditch by armed

Left: Fort Vaux after initial German bombardment.
Taylor Library

Centre: After the fort's recapture by the French.
Taylor Library

Bottom: Façade of Fort Vaux in 2008. *Author's collection*

bunkers set in the outer corners. Further improvements included three observation posts protected by heavy steel domes, a retractable gun turret for two short-barrelled 75mm guns and two Bourges Casemates, each armed with twin 75mm guns. By 1914 all these defensive elements were connected to the barracks by strong underground passages that allowed secure access at all times.

Disarmed in 1915, Fort Vaux was hastily re-armed after the start of the Verdun offensive and successfully resisted the first German assault in early March. A second attempt on the fort in May was also unsuccessful and further assaults were abandoned until the French had been cleared from the slopes below Forts Douaumont and Vaux. With these positions finally in German hands on 1 June, the commander of XV Corps, General von Deimling, ordered the assault on Fort Vaux to begin the following day. All night the heavy guns pounded the fort and at 3am the assault troops moved forward. It took them no time to reach the fort. The steep hillside to the north and east of the fort lay in dead ground to French guns and the nearest German trench was scarcely 150 metres away.

By now Fort Vaux was not as strong as it had once been. The months of shelling had damaged the gun bunkers, filled the ditch with stones and earth, blocked the main entrance with chunks of concrete and cracked the barracks. More worrying still, the water supply, which had been damaged in March, had not been repaired, and communication with the outside world depended on runners, blinker lamp or pigeons. The regular garrison had been swollen by such a mass of battlefield refugees that the new commander, Major Sylvain-Eugène Raynal, had difficulty in reaching his command post when he arrived to take up his duties.

Raynal, a regular soldier who had been badly wounded several times since the start of the war, had responded to a request for convalescent officers to take command of the forts. Arriving on 21 May, he immediately saw that the fort was too lightly armed to resist a determined infantry attack and could easily be cut off. When the bombardment began on

Major Raynal, commander of Fort Vaux. *H P von Müller's estate*

1 June, he realized that a major assault was imminent and, ordering barricades to be built in all the openings, he posted sentries and got the machine guns ready. As soon as the bombardment ceased on 2 June, men rushed out of the barracks but they were too late. The first German troops had raced to the ditch as the last shells were falling and while some units pushed around the outside in an attempt to encircle it, others crossed the ditch and scrambled on top, driving the defenders back with showers of grenades.

Unable to reach the superstructure, the French ran to the ditch bunkers and brought the ditches under heavy machine gun fire. The Germans tried various methods of knocking out these guns, including pumping smoke inside the bunkers and exploding sacks of hand grenades outside the gun embrasures, but the French fought back strongly and it was several hours before the Germans managed to gain control of the bunkers and remove the danger to the ditch.

Forced out of the bunkers, the French withdrew into the deep tunnels under the fort, where in the darknesss they built strong barricades backed by machine guns. With the Germans unable to enter the barracks any other way, it was in these tunnels – little more than 60 metres in length – that for the next five days the fight for Fort Vaux took place. Slowly, the Germans inched forward, methodically destroying each barricade with flame throwers, grenades and explosives. As each one fell, volunteers covered by machine guns firing just above their heads crawled forward to leap into the breach and hurl grenades at the attackers. Working on hands and knees with scraps of cloth tied over their faces, suffocated by dust and blackened by smoke, the defenders used fallen masonry, blocks of concrete, beams of wood, dismantled bedsteads or anything else they could find to build or repair the barricades. As the days went by the air filled with dust and fumes that spread back into the barracks, where they mixed with the growing stench of corpses and latrines. As the heat rose and the air grew thick, candles and lamps went out and men lay on the floor to breathe. In the tiny first-aid post, wounded men, some terribly burned, lay wherever they could, in filthy conditions and without proper medical attention.

And there was worse to come. On the third day of the siege, the sergeant in charge of water announced to Raynal that the cistern was almost empty. Unable to believe his ears Raynal at first suspected betrayal but he was assured that the fault lay in an inaccurate gauge. Horrified, he ordered that the remaining water should be preserved and sent out his last pigeon with the desperate message that they were

German postcard commemorating the 53rd Infantry Regiment, the first to reach Fort Vaux on 2 June 1916. *Author's collection*

holding on but reaching the end of their strength. The pigeon, which had to be coaxed into the air, finally took off for the Verdun citadel, where it arrived half asphyxiated and soon died (see Walk No. 10). No answer was received.

With thirst now the greatest enemy, Raynal decided that all superfluous men should leave the fort. They would be accompanied by a 19-year-old officer cadet named Léon Buffet, whose task was to get through to French lines, explain the situation and insist on immediate relief. On 5 June – the fourth night of the siege – Buffet and a handful of others somehow managed to scramble out of the fort and get back to French lines. Buffet explained the situation and, with relief promised for the following day, he volunteered to return to the fort with the news. Miraculously managing to avoid the German guns again, Buffet re-entered the fort where, in a fever of excitement, measures were taken to support the attack. But when the long-awaited French artillery barrage began on 6 June the shells passed harmlessly overhead, exploding some distance away. Powerless to ask Fort Souville to shorten the range – in the smoke and dust of the bombardment, Raynal's blinker signals went unseen – the besieged garrison could only watch with sinking hearts as the relief attempt failed once again.

With morale at its lowest ebb, Raynal toured the fort. By now everyone was tortured with thirst. Since 4 June all his men had

Runners passing through the ruins of Fort Vaux. *Taylor Library*

received was one small cup of muddy, stinking water and Raynal found men slumped unconscious in the corridors or desperately trying to relieve their thirst by licking moisture off the walls or drinking their own urine. Appalled by what he saw and realizing that no relief would come, Raynal decided that Fort Vaux had done its duty. Blinking out a final message to Fort Souville, of which only a few, incomprehensible words were picked up, he drew up a letter for the German commander, which was handed through one of the barricades.

In the early hours of 7 June the Germans entered the fort. The surrender was signed and in silence the survivors – almost 600 officers and men and a little dog – made their way between two ranks of Germans, who presented arms. There were just enough fit men to carry the wounded. Stupefied, the Germans watched as the filthy and bloody survivors staggered past them into the open air and threw themselves down at the first shell hole to drink madly at the muddy water.

Later that day Raynal was taken to meet the commander of the 50th Division, to whom he made it clear that thirst had defeated the garrison, not the Germans. The following day he met Crown Prince William of

Plaque commemorating Fort Vaux's carrier pigeons. On 4 June 1916 the last of the fort's four pigeons left Fort Vaux for the Verdun Citadel carrying a desperate appeal for relicf. *Author's collection*

Major Raynal (centre) after the capture of Fort Vaux. *Taylor Library*

Germany, who congratulated him on the fort's brave resistance and, as Raynal had no sword, offered him the sword of another French officer. Not wishing to explain that he had arrived at Fort Vaux armed only with a walking stick, Raynal accepted the sword and left for captivity. He received the Legion of Honour for his part in defending the fort and returned to the army after the war, retiring in 1929 with the rank of colonel.

'We have got Fort Vaux', cried a jubilant German to a French soldier captured below Fort Douaumont. 'Wonderful,' retorted the prisoner. 'And have you also got Souville?' They had not. Furthermore, after four months of desperate and costly struggle, the battle for Fort Souville had not even begun.

The walk

This walk begins at the modern village of Vaux-devant-Damloup. To

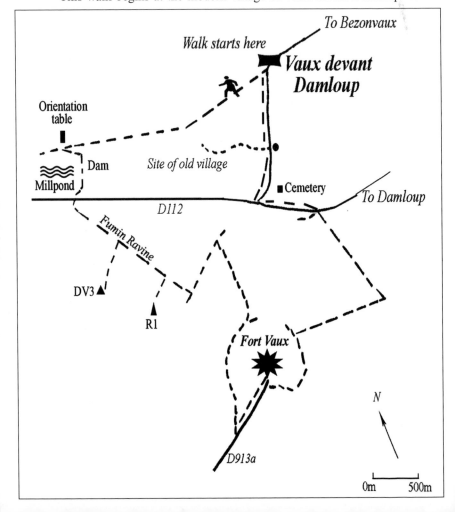

reach the start of the walk, take the D603 from Verdun towards Etain. (NB: On the IGN maps, this road is still numbered N3.) The road crosses the Meuse Heights and drops down to a roundabout close to the village of Eix. At the roundabout turn left on the D24 towards Damloup. Drive through Damloup and at the crossroads with the D112 turn left towards Verdun. Continue until you reach a cemetery on the right-hand side and turn right just beyond it following the sign to *Vaux village détruit*. Drive towards the chapel ahead, ignoring the small monument on the right of the road that commemorates the destroyed village and is dealt with at the end of the walk. Park and face the entrance to the chapel.

The original village of Vaux-devant-Damloup, which is now totally destroyed, was situated on the other side of this valley and the modern village occupies a new site. In 1914 the ridge in front of you was the site of four fieldworks that made up the Hardaumont defensive complex. Direct access to the Hardaumont sector was provided by Grand Houyers Ravine, a steep valley that runs uphill from the left of

Post-war postcard of the French naval gun in Grand Houyers ravine.

Author's collection

the chapel. The valley was the site of a French 24cm naval gun – now destroyed – so positioned as to control the railway line and roads on the plain to your right. The gun's existence is recalled in the name of the street to the left of the chapel – *Allée de la Pièce de Marine*: Naval Gun Way.

To start the walk, follow the wide track on the left of the clock tower which is signposted *Monument aux Morts de Vaux* and *Etang de Vaux, Table d'Orientation 800 mètres*. The track runs along the embankment for the *Tacot*, the light railway that ran from Verdun to Montmedy close to the Belgian border. Passing the village war memorial on the right, continue to the orientation table, which is approximately one kilometre ahead. The table has an interesting sketch of the area as seen by German balloon observers before the assault of 21 February 1916. At that time, Forts Douaumont and Vaux would have been visible from where you are standing. The adjacent small memorial records the actions of 126 officers and men of the 1st Battalion of Chasseurs à Pied (light infantry), who died in the final successful German assault on the original village of Vaux on 31 March 1916. Note the communication trench running down the hillside between the orientation table and the Chasseurs memorial.

Now face the other side of the valley. Fort Vaux stands in the trees at the top of the hill in front of you. Below you is the *Etang de Vaux*, the former village millpond, which at the time of writing has been drained. The original village stood in the trees to your left front. The Germans first attacked Vaux at the end of February 1916 but it was the

Where Vaux village once stood. *Taylor Library*

Vaux pond. *Taylor Library*

end of March before the ruined houses were under their control. Even then the French held a number of strong positions both here and on the opposite hillside, from which they were able to block the German movement across the valley and uphill towards the fort.

From the orientation table, go down the steps following the sign marked *Abris d'Infanterie DV3, DV4, Fort de Vaux 1200m* and cross the dam to the other side of the valley, then stop and look back. Having cleared the French out of the village at the end of March, it took the Germans another two months to gain control of the dam, which was the shortest route across the valley and the only firm path through an area of impassable marsh. Knowing its importance to the Germans, the French kept the dam under constant fire and, to the unfortunate men who had to cross it, the fearful route was known as the *Todespfad* or Death Path. On all sides the ground was strewn with material jettisoned in their haste to reach the other side, including wounded, for whom it was too dangerous to stop. Guy Dussumier Latour, whose death is commemorated halfway across the dam, was a pilot with the French 1st Aviation Group. His name is recorded on a plaque in the Vaux section of the Ossuary.

Fumin Ravine DV3, DV4, R1

Now follow the path that runs uphill past the information board. Continue for approximately 400 metres and stop at the sign reading *Abri d'Infanterie DV3, 200m*. You are now on the western side of Fumin Ravine, a vitally important valley that offered the Germans direct access between the old village and Fort Vaux. Fighting for this ravine – the site of numerous French infantry strongpoints – began

77

Shelters and gun positions were subjected to such fierce bombardment that they came to resemble caves in natural rock.
Taylor Library

Infantry shelter DV4.
Author's collection

immediately after the fall of the village and it soon became a place of horror. The Germans quickly managed to establish themselves on the opposite side of the valley but violent resistance prevented them for two months from reaching the side where you now stand.

Now turn right and follow the path to infantry shelter DV3 (marked by a solid green circle on a white background). The path starts by following an old communication trench but soon leaves it and runs uphill through an area of stunted trees, endless shell holes and trenches. When you reach the shelter, face the front but do not attempt to enter it.

The strongpoints in this ravine included three concrete entrenchments and two strong shelters. This one housed half a company in two rooms whose entrances were protected by a massive blast wall. There was a kitchen in a third room and an outside latrine. The lower floor contained a water cistern and the whole area was surrounded by barbed wired. Having finally captured this shelter on 1 June 1916, the Germans cut an exit through the rear wall

to facilitate access from the direction of the mill pond. They also drove a tunnel into Fumin Ravine from the water cistern, possibly to connect with the many dugouts excavated there. From the left-hand end of DV3 a shallow communication trench running for some 50 metres leads to the ruins of a small searchlight shelter. It is not clear whether a searchlight was ever installed here.

Now return to your original path and turn right uphill. At the sign for *Abri d'Infanterie DV4, 125m,* turn right. Follow the path to the ruined shelter, then stop and face downhill. You are now at the top of Fumin Ravine. Although the Germans quickly established themselves in positions around the hillside to your right, they were unable to cross to the other side of the ravine, which was commanded by this shelter and a long concrete entrenchment named R1. One of many similar entrenchments built before the war, R1 – which stood to the right of the shelter and has totally disappeared – comprised a stone parapet approximately two metres high and 150 metres long. It was connected to DV4 by a communication trench. During April and May 1916, the Germans managed to drive saps to within 50 metres of R1 but their repeated attacks on the position were unsuccessful and by the beginning of June the ground here was littered with corpses, smashed debris and blood-stained belongings.

During the siege of Fort Vaux, R1 was held by a company of the 101st Infantry commanded by Captain Charles Delvert, whose account of their experience is a classic of Verdun literature. During that crucial period R1 was not only in the closest possible contact with the Germans but in the direct line of their advance on the fort. Unable to sleep for a moment, tortured by thirst and, as if that were not enough, shelled by their own artillery with devastating results, Delvert and his dwindling band of men held off repeated German attacks from 31 May to 5 June 1916. These assaults were so costly for the Germans that further attacks were called off and it was only after Fort Vaux had surrendered that R1 was taken.

From DV4 return to the main path and turn right. Henri Waechter, a machine gunner with the 124th Infantry, who is commemorated on the monument by the path, was reinterred after the war in front of the Ossuary (plot 8178). At the top of the hill, turn left on a wide forest road following the sign for *Fort de Vaux 1000m.* On the IGN maps this path is named the *Chemin de la Vau Régnier.* Continue for approximately 250 metres, noting the extremely extensive view over the plain ahead, and turn right at forest block 514, following the *Sentier de Vaux.* The path now rises to the top of the plateau on which Fort Vaux stands. After roughly 250 metres you will reach a junction of four

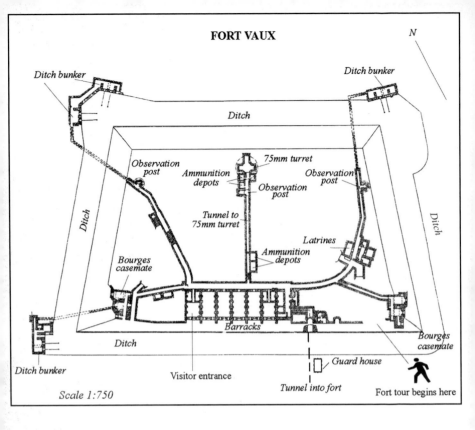

Ditch bunker

Ditch bunker

Ditch

Observation post

Ammunition depots

75mm turret

Observation post

Observation post

Ditch

Tunnel to 75mm turret

Ditch

Latrines

Bourges casemate

Ammunition depots

Barracks

Bourges casemate

Ditch

Ditch bunker

Visitor entrance

Guard house

Tunnel into fort

Fort tour begins here

Scale 1:750

tracks, with block 508 ahead of you. Take the right-hand track, following the sign showing a solid green circle on a white arrow. Follow the track to the road (D913a) and turn left. A further 250 metres will bring you to the car park at Fort Vaux. The long concrete structure in front of you as you approach the fort is the former barracks. To visit the fort, turn left along the front of the barracks to the visitor entrance.

A brief tour of Fort Vaux
The exterior

The present façade of Fort Vaux bears little relation to its original appearance. The barracks were originally protected by a wall almost high enough to cover the blocked-up archways that you see today. This was pierced by a row of gun embrasures and also by the 'peacetime' gate into the fort, which was protected by a drawbridge. The 'wartime' gate – an underground tunnel – is still to be seen in the grassy dip between the two parking areas. The original gates are still in place but the tunnel is blocked by debris. The thick concrete covering on the façade of the barracks was added in 1889 but the blockhouses built

French infantry assaulting a Geman position. *Taylor Library*

into the archways date from the fort's recapture by the French in November 1916. During the German occupation the original archways were destroyed by shelling and the gaping holes blocked up by massive walls of sandbags. The apparently undamaged concrete bunkers at either end of the barracks are the Bourges Casemates. Smashed during the battle, they were restored during the 1930s to provide back-up for the Maginot Line.

From the front of the barracks, follow the path that starts between the 'pigeon' commemorative plaque and the Bourges Casemate and climbs to the top of the fort. Stand by the flagpole with your back to the approach road to the fort. From here you have a clear view of the damage caused by shellfire during the Battle of Verdun. Fort Douaumont and the Ossuary stand on the ridge that forms the horizon to your left front. To your right, the views that stretch for miles over the

The destroyed 75mm gun turret. *Author's collection*

Woëvre Plain leave no doubt about the importance of Fort Vaux for observation and defence.

Directly in front of you is the destroyed 75mm gun turret. Follow the footpath to the turret, passing the light steel observation dome that rather resembles an enormous medieval helmet. Walk up to the top of the turret and face the ditch, which is immediately in front of you. The heavy steel observation dome set in the concrete served this turret, to which it was connected by speaking tube.

Between June and November 1916, Fort Vaux was less than one kilometre from the front line, which ran to your left rear. For the Germans it formed a vital strongpoint and centre of resistance, offering shelter, food, rest and basic medical facilities for thousands of men. The French counter-offensive of 24 October 1916 failed to retake this fort but left the Germans in no doubt that it could not be held much longer. As a result, it was evacuated in the early hours of 2 November. By this time it was a smoking ruin. In compliance with an order to destroy as much of it as possible, German pioneers had blown up ten of the fort's vital organs, including this turret. The honour of lighting the fuse went to the pioneer commander, Captain Rosencrantz. The steel cupola that protected the guns was blown in the air and fell where it now lies with pieces of the massive turret rim all around. The French subsequently turned the turret into a machine gun position. Further machine gun posts replaced the destroyed observation posts on the eastern and western shoulders of the fort.

Now follow the footpath down to the cupola and face the ditch. The bunkers that caused the Germans so many hours of trouble on 2 June 1916 are to your left and right. During their occupation of the fort the Germans tunnelled out from the bunker to your right in order to create new, secure access at some distance from the fort. However, the tunnel was never finished and the workings were destroyed before the fort was evacuated. There is no access to either of the bunkers but visitors wishing to have a closer look can make their way into the ditch and then walk round to the visitor entrance. Visitors who do not wish to go down into the ditch should return to the visitor entrance at the front of the fort.

The interior

The visit begins in the entrance hall, which contains a selection of books and postcards and some interesting memorabilia of French veterans of the siege. Continue through the 'museum' – the first room – into the main corridor. The stairs immediately in front of you as you enter the corridor lead down to the former water cisterns and one of the underground tunnels excavated after the battle. Turn right along the main corridor. The entrance to be seen behind a gate on the left leads to the 75mm gun turret, which is inaccessible. During their occupation of the fort the Germans used the 75mm turret as a signalling station. The twin gun barrels were used to concentrate the beams of light from acetylene signalling lamps that flashed messages to a receiving station to the north-east of the fort. The tomb to be seen at the bottom of the steps is symbolic and represents all the men who were buried in the fort before it was surrendered. Their bodies were covered in quicklime, chunks of which are to be seen on the shelf to the right of the tomb entrance.

Continue to Commandant Raynal's command post, which is a little further along on the right, and turn right just beyond it. The first room on the right is the infirmary. A short distance further along on the left a grating covers a hole that has been broken through the original stone wall of the fort. Visible through the hole is the concrete layer with which the fort was covered in 1889. The gap between stone and concrete was originally filled with a metre-thick layer of sand that was designed to absorb the shock of shells hitting the fort. The Germans used the sand for building and repair work in the fort during their occupation.

Continue to the fort commandant's bedroom, telephone exchange and the pigeon loft. At the bottom of the flight of stairs by the pigeon loft a deep pit leads to the tunnel system excavated by the French after the fort was retaken in November 1916. The system included a well and an 800-metre-long tunnel with multiple access branches and emergency exits. The exit on the left of the shaft leads to a small external blockhouse built after the French retook the fort, while the blocked up tunnel entrance on the other side of the shaft leads to the 'wartime' gate. The red line on the walls indicates that this part of the fort was strong enough to resist heavy shelling.

Return up the stairs and turn right, then turn right again through the iron gates following *Coffre nord-est* and noting the damage to the walls and ceiling, which was caused by the German attempts to destroy the fort from the inside at the end of October 1916. It makes plain the vast thickness of the concrete layer that the French poured on the fort in 1889. Continue to the walls that block the corridor. The flight of stairs on the right just before you reach them leads to the eastern Bourges Casemate, which is inaccessible. Continue past the walls and go down the short flight of steps. On the left are the latrines. Captured by the Germans on 5 June, conditions here became so appalling that they could only be used with breathing apparatus. On the right are the powder magazines, one of which still has an original door. Beyond the

Façade of Fort Vaux after the Battle of Verdun. *H P von Müller's estate*

A view along the eastern ditch of Fort Vaux showing the first bunker to be attacked by the Germans. *Author's collection*

powder magazines the corridor that leads to the ditch bunker is inaccessible.

Now return to the main corridor and when you reach it walk straight ahead, passing the entrance to the cisterns. The small chapel to be seen on the right is situated at the entrance to the corridor through which the Germans entered the fort on 7 June. Continue straight ahead into a long corridor that was rebuilt during the 1930s. This leads to the only accessible Bourges Casemate, a strong concrete bunker originally armed with two quick-firing 75mm fortress guns but disarmed in 1915 and re-armed with machine guns. There was an observation post adjacent to the chambers, magazines on the lower floor and an underground passage from this casemate to the ditch bunker opposite. It is today the haunt of swallows, whose noisy chirping fills the air during spring and summer.

Return to Vaux village
At the end of the visit, return through the entrance hall and turn left along the front of the barracks. Pass the plaques commemorating the defenders of Fort Vaux and the pigeon and walk towards the furthest point of the car park. Ahead of you is a track barred by a wooden pole. Pass the pole and follow the track, which bends to the left. Ignoring other paths entering to left or right, continue until you reach a T-junction and turn right downhill with block 514 on your left and a

concrete telegraph pole on your right. Follow the telegraph poles down to the bottom of the hill noting, once it gets really steep, trenches running across the hillside from left to right. This hill was of extreme importance to the Germans during the Battle of Verdun as it was sheltered from French artillery fire. This allowed them to establish themselves within 150 metres of this side of the fort before the siege began and it also provided a protected site for camps, dumps, first-aid posts and anything else that was needed.

Continue to the bottom of the hill and at a T-junction with a level track turn left. Follow the track until you reach the road (D112) and then turn left again. Walk along the road for a short distance, then turn round and look back. The vast extent of the view over the plain makes immediately clear the pre-war importance of the ridges on either side of you for defence, observation and signalling. Continue past the cemetery and turn right at the sign marked *Vaux, village détruit* to return to the chapel. Halfway along the road on the right is the monument to the destroyed village, with the memorial to the church beyond it at the field edge. The old village was actually situated on the left of the road and visitors wishing to visit the site should follow the path that passes the barrier opposite the monument. This ends close to the site of the former village church and a small monument to a workman killed by an explosion in 1951. After visiting the atmospheric site, return to the road and walk back to the chapel.

German prisoners stretcher wounded away during the fighting.

Taylor Library

Walk No. 5

THE GERMAN OFFENSIVE OF 23 JUNE 1916
PART 1 – THIAUMONT AND FROIDETERRE

Duration: two hours.
Distance: five kilometres.

This walk covers the assault on the Thiaumont and Froideterre fieldworks by units of the 1st Bavarian Infantry Division on 23 June 1916. It is covered by IGN maps 3112 ET and Blue Series 3212 Ouest. There is a short steep section on the approach to Froideterre and another of approximately 400 metres at the end of the walk but the rest is either level or downhill. It is likely to be muddy throughout the year.

Warning: The positions covered by this walk were seriously damaged during the Battle of Verdun and visitors should not try to enter any of them. At Froideterre, do not try to cross the ditch, which is still a mass of picket posts and wire.

The events

With Fort Vaux finally in their hands, the Germans could push forward against the last major obstacle on the road to Verdun. This was a two-kilometre-long crest that ran like the crossbar of a letter H between the two ridges on which stood Forts Douaumont and Vaux. Once over the crossbar – the site of the charmingly named village of Fleury – there would only be one remaining obstacle on the path to Verdun. This was a lower height topped by two older forts – Belleville and St. Michel – which the German High Command did not consider capable of offering serious resistance. However, attacking the crossbar was fraught with danger, as it was flanked by numerous positions from which the French could pour fire into any German advance. The most important of these were Fort Souville, which commanded the southern approach to the crossbar, Thiaumont, a small fieldwork dominating the northern approach, and Froideterre, a major fieldwork situated on the hillside beyond Thiaumont with commanding views over Fleury. While Thiaumont was small and mounted no artillery, Froideterre, heavily armed with three revolving gun turrets, would be a more difficult nut to crack.

However dangerous the operation, it had to be undertaken. With Germany's forces stretched to the limit on the Western Front, required to support her Austro-Hungarian ally on the Eastern Front and facing

The entrance to Fort Belleville. *Author's collection*

an imminent Allied offensive on the Somme, General von Falkenhayn had to make a last attempt to bring matters at Verdun to a close.

The date he chose for the final offensive was 23 June. As on previous occasions, the heavy artillery was to crush all physical obstacles. On the right, following a swift blow against Thiaumont by units of the 1st Bavarian Division, the elite Alpenkorps would sweep through Fleury and continue towards Belleville ridge. On the left, where the line was further back, an earlier start would allow it to be straightened before units of the 103rd Division pushed forward towards Fort Souville. If successful, the offensive would bring the Germans so close to Verdun that the city would become untenable.

General Krafft von Dellmensingen, commander of the Alpenkorps.
H P von Müller's estate

Success depended on silencing the French batteries, which had on so many previous occasions prevented the exploitation of an initially successful assault. To do so – and, in addition, to prevent the arrival of reserves – a new weapon was to be used: phosgene, a gas against which

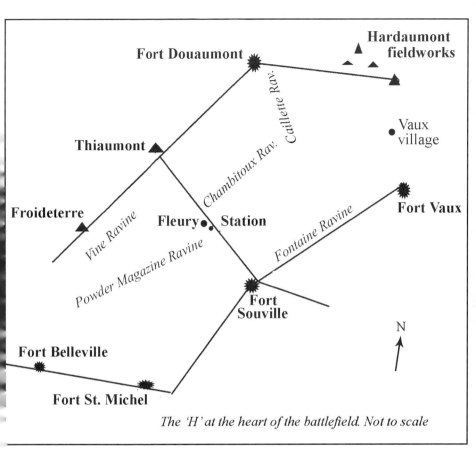

The 'H' at the heart of the battlefield. Not to scale

French gas masks offered inadequate protection. Known from the painted marking on the shells as Green Cross gas, phosgene was not intended for use on the French front lines but on the forts, fieldworks and batteries that supported them. The hope was that if these could be knocked out for even a short time, the Germans would be able to seize all the important positions that blocked their approach to Verdun.

On 21 June, with the German line roughly 500 metres from Thiaumont and two kilometres from Fort Souville, a colossal bombardment smashed into the French positions on the Right Bank, destroying shelters and communications and throwing up such thick clouds of dust that visibility came down to a few metres. The French batteries were soon reduced to a horrible chaos of shattered guns, smashed equipment and sticky, blood-soaked earth. During the afternoon, the three German army corps on the Right Bank of the Meuse began to move forward, but the long bombardment had warned the French of the impending assault and the attack was stopped. However, the French situation was critical. It was clear that a major

French guns such as these
had to be neutralized on
23 June. *Taylor Library*

Above: 155mm gun.

Left: 75mm gun.

German offensive was in preparation and all across the front French commanders were calling for reinforcements. In Verdun, anxiety began to reach panic levels and hurried evacuation preparations began, with all non-essential services being sent to the rear.

The phosgene bombardment began late on 22 June. During the night, gas clouds formed in the ravines, delaying the arrival of supplies and reinforcements. They spread to the batteries, where frenzied horses plunged and reared, breaking their harness and running amok. Retching and coughing, the gunners rushed to put on their gas masks but found they were not protected against the new weapon. As dawn broke, the softening up process began again, raising the level of fire to apocalyptic levels. The earth shook and shuddered as shells howled over the French lines, smashing the front lines and throwing up huge fountains of earth and smoke. Powerless under the torrent of metal, the French defenders – the 129th

Early protection against German gas attacks.
Taylor Library

Division on the left, the 130th Division in the centre and the 12th Division on the right – crouched in any shelter they could find, waiting for the attack.

Thiaumont and Froideterre

It came at 6am the next morning. On the German right, the unit entrusted with the task of taking Thiaumont, Froideterre and the intervening positions was the *Regiment König Ludwig No. 10*, the oldest regiment in the Bavarian Army. By now the battlefield was a wasteland. The months of shelling had annihilated shelters and trenches, wiped fields and villages off the map and left a chaotic landscape that was filled with debris and haunted by rats. The Bavarians' front lines, which had seen heavy fighting during the previous month, were an appalling sight, with helmets, packs and ammunition scattered everywhere and corpses in all stages of decomposition. The sight of it, and the constant earth-shaking bombardment, so affected the men's nerves that some units moved off before the appointed time. Accompanied by pioneers and Jägers they stormed down the ridge to the Thiaumont fieldwork, bursting out of the clouds of smoke and dust to take the French by surprise. After two days

91

The barracks at Froideterre. *Author's collection*

of obliterating bombardment with high explosives and gas, Thiaumont's defenders, a battalion of Chasseurs, were exhausted and their commander was out of action. They fought until the battalion was destroyed and the Bavarian wave washed over them. Leaving a unit in place to organize the captured position, the Bavarians streamed on down the ridge, sweeping French resistance aside and reaching 'Four Chimneys', an underground shelter for reserves with four ventilation shafts. While some men attacked the shelter, others pressed on towards Froideterre.

Finding it was not easy. While Froideterre was clear enough on the map, the months of shelling had obliterated all reference points in the landscape and it was some time before Lieutenant Karl Ludwig, the leader of the Bavarian assault group, spotted a gun turret among the mounds of earth flung up by the shells. Assuming that the fieldwork would be a mass of rubble he ordered his small group forward. To their surprise, they were met by violent fire.

The fieldwork had survived the bombardment well. Its three rotating turrets – two mounting machine guns and a third housing twin 75s – were only superficially damaged and while conditions inside were not perfect, the garrison was well supplied and morale was high. When an observer reported seeing the Bavarians at Thiaumont, Froideterre's commander, Captain Robert Dartigues, realized that an attack was imminent. Sending some men to free a jammed machine gun turret and others to set up guns to cover the courtyard, he ordered the 75s to be loaded with shrapnel and calmly allowed the German advance to continue. As soon as the Bavarians appeared, the machine guns covering the courtyard went into action. Forced to withdraw, they worked around the back of barracks and scrambled on the roof, where they threw hand grenades into any openings they could find. As they did so, they were seen by observers at Fort Douaumont, who promptly announced that Froideterre was in Bavarian hands.

But it was not to be. The hand grenades ignited a stock of signal rockets inside the barracks and thick smoke billowed out, causing panic to both attackers and defenders. Inside, the French rushed to put out the fire before it ignited an ammunition store. Outside, fearing a repeat of the terrible explosion that had occurred in Fort Douaumont in May, Ludwig ordered his men to pull back. By the time they realized that the fieldwork would not explode, it was too late. With the machine gun turret in action again and the 75s firing shrapnel at short range, the Bavarians were unable to advance.

Ludwig realized that while his small group would not be able to take Froideterre, the fieldwork could certainly be captured by properly equipped pioneers and storm troops. He sent out a call for reinforcements but by now the French batteries had recovered from the gas attack and were laying a curtain of fire between the German front lines and the rear. This prevented the arrival of all but a handful of men and, fearing that they would be cut off, Ludwig decided to withdraw. In the early hours of 24 June the little group – by now reduced to fifteen men – set off towards German lines. As they did so, they ran into the French. In an exchange of fire Ludwig was wounded and his men were taken prisoner as fresh French units thrust along the ridge, pushing the Bavarians several hundred metres back.

That day – 23 June – was a costly one for the 10th Bavarian Infantry, who lost 50 per cent of their effectives in the attack on Froideterre ridge. Even though they captured Thiaumont, their failure to take the Froideterre fieldwork left the French with controlling views over Fleury ridge and the open slopes below it. For the rest of the summer, not a mouse could move in the Fleury sector without French observers at Froideterre calling down an immediate artillery barrage on the men crouching desperately below.

The walk

This walk begins at the Ossuary. To reach the start of the walk take the D603 from Verdun towards Etain. (NB: on the IGN maps, this road is still numbered N3.) Follow the road uphill from Verdun and turn left at the junction with the D913, following signs to *Champ de Bataille 14–18*. At the crossroads with the D112, continue ahead, following signs to *Mémorial de Verdun* and *Ossuaire*. At the next crossroads, drive uphill to the Ossuary car park, passing the Jewish memorial on the left. Park and walk back towards the Jewish memorial. Just before you reach it, turn right by the sign reading *Ouvrage de Thiaumont et PC 118*. At the wooden bench, walk towards the *Ouvrage de Thiaumont*. Follow the footpath to the ruined fieldwork and walk up to the orientation table, avoiding the remaining reinforcing bars and picket posts.

Ouvrage de Thiaumont

This little fieldwork is the heart of the battle. Built where the Douaumont ridge meets the Fleury crossbar, it controlled the approach to Fleury from the north and offered sweeping views in all directions.

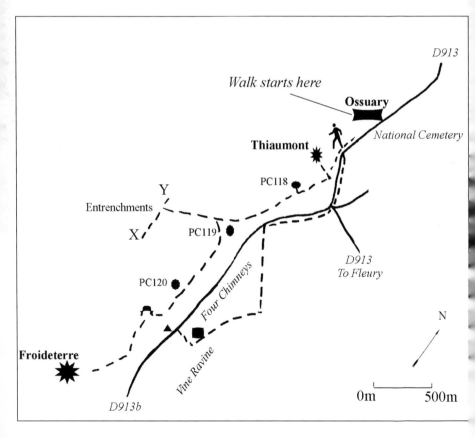

French assaults on positions such as Thiaumont were costly in officers and men. *Taylor Library*

It was originally a small concrete-covered work armed with a retractable machine gun turret and two 75mm guns housed in a Bourges Casemate. There was an armoured observation post, a small shelter for the garrison and, surrounding the whole work, a ditch protected by a high railing and wire. Like the other defences in the sector, Thiaumont was disarmed in 1915 and it was later downgraded to a shelter. However, once captured by the Germans, it became the focus of intense shelling and repeated counter-attacks. It was popularly said to have changed hands many times, but the French Official History makes it clear that although all the French assaults on Thiaumont were extremely costly in officers and men, none was successful until 3 August, when the French managed to recapture it for a few days. However, it soon returned to German hands, where it remained until 24 October 1916.

From the middle of August 1916, the front lines ran less than 500 metres to the south of Thiaumont and by October it was completely destroyed. The orientation table stands on the smashed Bourges Casemate. All that remains of the machine gun turret and observation post are the pivot for the guns, the battered observation dome and a cluster of reinforcing bars. Of the shelter, wire and railing there is no trace at all. Although softened by greenery and the passage of time, Thiaumont remains a permanent memorial to the unimaginable fury of the shelling and the horrors of the summer of 1916.

Now walk back towards the Jewish Memorial. At the wooden bench, turn right towards *Rety Y 1000 mètres, Rety X 1400 mètres*. Continue ahead, noting on the left the plaque commemorating Pierre Teilhard de Chardin, an influential Jesuit priest and philosopher, whose wartime service as a front-line stretcher bearer with the *4ième Régiment Mixte de Zouaves et Tirailleurs* included several tours of duty in this area. At the sign for *PC 118*, turn right.

Retranchements X and Y, PC 119

PC 118 (the name means Command Post 118) is one of three identical shelters between Froideterre and Thiaumont. Their design is described in Walk No. 4. During the battle these shelters, which were often the only recognizable sights in the devastated landscape, served as

All that is left of the Bourges Casemate at Thiaumont. *Author's collection*

A post-war view of the Thiaumont fieldwork. *Author's collection*

The same view of the Thiaumont fieldwork in 2007. Note the Ossuary tower in the background. *Author's collection*

PC 118. *Author's collection*

command, observation and first-aid posts, refuges and signalling stations. From here, messages were sent by blinker lamp if the weather was clear, by telephone if shelling had not cut the lines, by carrier pigeon or, if all else failed, by runner. Always overflowing with men, dark, insanitary and under constant bombardment, they were the only safe places in a landscape of horror. This one has been so heavily shelled that the massive blast wall protecting the entrance to the shelter's two rooms has been completely destroyed. The crosses on the top commemorate two men who died here at the beginning of June 1916.

Now return to the track and turn right. At the junction with a wide forest road approximately 50 metres further on, continue straight ahead following *Sentier de Froideterre, PC 119 400 mètres* and keep on until you reach two brown wooden signposts on the left of the track. These indicate *Sentier de Froideterre* to the left and point ahead to *Retranchement Y 400 mètres, Retranchement X 800 mètres.* Continue towards the entrenchments. The distant skyline that comes into view ahead of you is the Mort-Homme, from where German observers had devastatingly clear views of the movement of French troops on this hillside.

98

Retranchement Y is on the right of the track while *Retranchement X*, which is considerably bigger, is situated a couple of hundred metres into the wood on the left. When they were built, these entrenchments enjoyed uninterrupted views towards the River Meuse and the Left Bank and controlled the routes between the river and this ridge. They consisted of a long stone or concrete parapet that was divided by buttresses into recesses in which troops could take shelter. Captured by the Germans on 23 June 1916, these entrenchments were soon recaptured and remained front-line positions throughout the summer.

From the entrenchments, return along the forest road to the two brown wooden signs that you saw

Retranchement X. *Author's collection*

previously. Turn right following *Sentier de Froideterre, Abris bétonnés 500m, PC 119 400 mètres* and make your way down to the front of the shelter. The plaque to the left of the entrance proudly recalls the heroic fighting that took place in this area during the Battle of Verdun and the part played by the *4th Régiment Mixte de Zouaves et Tirailleurs* in the French counter-offensive of October 1916. The monuments on the top to battalion commander Charles Ridouard and the officers and men of the 5th Battalion, 317th Infantry, who died in a fire here on 31 July 1916, commemorate an event that was not uncommon in places where so many heavily armed men were crammed together.

PC 120, gun battery

Now go down to the track by the information plinth and turn right along the *Sentier de Froideterre*. Passing *PC 120*, which is in good condition and gives an idea of the original strength and size of these infantry shelters, continue to the gun battery that stands some 50 metres further along on the right. Between 1875 and 1914, a total of 110 batteries were constructed at Verdun. This is one of the earlier types, with platforms for four guns separated by protective mounds of earth. Ammunition was stored in the niches in front of the guns, and

PC 120. *Author's collection*

the small shelter offered protection for the crews and served as a command post. Only two of the gun platforms have been excavated; the other two remain buried in undergrowth.

From the battery, continue to the road and turn uphill following *Ouvrage de Froideterre 300 mètres.* Immediately in front of you on reaching the parking area is the green-painted 75mm gun turret. Walk up to the grey-painted dome on top of the turret and face the car park.

Ouvrage de Froideterre

The thick forest that covers the battlefield today makes it impossible to understand the importance of this fieldwork in 1916. Situated at the end of a long bare ridge that offered extensive views in all directions, Froideterre was in direct communication with many other forts on both sides of the River Meuse and controlled the road out of Verdun to the north. Building began here in the late 1880s. The barracks, which includes one of Froideterre's two machine gun turrets, is the long building to your left. The second machine gun turret is to your right and the flat roof visible beyond it is the Bourges Casemate, which originally housed two 75mm fortress guns. Each turret was connected with an armoured observation post and the whole work was surrounded by an iron railing set in the middle of a deep ditch. When first built, there was no internal communication between the various blocks. An attempt to link them underground during the summer of

1916 was only partially successful and it was 1917 before deep tunnels were driven between them. These tunnels are inaccessible today.

Between June and October 1916, Froideterre was never more than 1,200 metres from the front line, and during that time it formed a vital command and observation post, signalling station and shelter for reserves. The first-aid post was always busy. Many operations were carried out here and the dead were buried in shell holes in the courtyard. Examined by military engineers after the battle, Froideterre was found to have resisted the bombardment surprisingly well. The wire and railing in the ditch had been destroyed and the machine gun turret in the barracks was out of action but the other turrets and the Bourges Casemate were in working order. Repairs were carried out in 1917, with further refurbishment in the early 1930s when the Maginot Line was under construction. On 15 June 1940, Froideterre fell to the Germans after a brief fight. The cluster of impacts to be seen on the cupola of the 75mm gun turret occurred on that occasion.

Ammunition Depot, Four Chimneys

From Froideterre, walk down the approach road to the junction with the D913b and turn left. A few metres beyond the junction a sign on the left reading *Dépôt de munitions* indicates the entrance to one of the four ammunition depots on this hillside. Continue to the sign reading *Abri Caverne des Quatre Cheminées* (Four Chimneys shelter) and turn right. Walk down to the 'chimneys', then stop and look directly ahead. The high clump of trees on the skyline immediately opposite you marks the site of Fort Souville, a mere two kilometres away. The skyline to your left is Fleury ridge. It is easy to see how, with no trees to block the view in 1916, Froideterre and Souville controlled all movement on and below Fleury ridge. The valley below you is Vine Ravine. One of the major French supply routes on the Right Bank, it was used throughout the battle by troops coming into the Thiaumont and Fleury sectors.

Four Chimneys shelter, a brick-lined cavern 70 metres long, was built to provide accommodation for reserves. On 23 June 1916 it housed, in addition to two brigade staffs and two regimental staffs, a substantial number of exhausted and gassed men, wounded, stretcher bearers and doctors. As the Bavarians approached, one of the brigade commanders, Colonel de Susbielle, desperately alerted his reserves. Although they were not far away, reaching the shelter meant passing through Vine Ravine, which was under violent bombardment and filled with gas. It took several hours of superhuman effort before the reserves reached the besieged shelter and, yelling and shouting, drove the Germans back at the point of the bayonet. Like Froideterre, Four Chimneys remained in French hands for the remainder of the battle. The 8th Battalion of the Moroccan Colonial Infantry was based here for the French counter-offensive of 24 October 1916, which succeeded in retaking Fort Douaumont (see Walk No. 8).

Return to the Ossuary

From the entrance to Four Chimneys, walk downhill to the monument to Pierre de Cazalis de Fondouce, who fell at Froideterre on 8 August 1916. Turn left here, following the sign for *Sentier de la Poudrière, Village détruit de Fleury 1850m*. Follow this path for approximately 300 metres until you reach a T-junction, then turn left uphill (do not follow the *Poudrière* path, which turns right). Continue to the D913b and turn right along the road to return to the Ossuary.

French infantry attacking. *Taylor Library*

102

Walk No. 6
THE GERMAN OFFENSIVE OF 23 JUNE 1916
PART 2 – THE BAVARIANS AT FLEURY

Duration: three hours, not including a museum visit.
Distance: eight kilometres.

This walk covers the attack on Fleury ridge by the Alpenkorps on 23 June 1916 and may include a visit to the Verdun Memorial museum. It is covered by IGN maps 3112 ET and Blue Series 3212 Ouest. The return journey involves an uphill section of approximately one kilometre on the *Chemin d'Hardaumont* but the rest is either level or downhill.

NB: Visitors who have not previously read Walk No. 5 should begin by reading the first six paragraphs of the Events section of that walk before beginning this one, as they form a general introduction to the attack on Fleury.

Warning: Visitors should stick to the paths and should not attempt to enter any of the structures described here.

The events

The unit responsible for taking the ridge topped by the prettily named village of Fleury-devant-Douaumont was the Alpenkorps. This was a highly rated body of hardened troops – Bavarian except for one Prussian Jäger regiment – with experience of mountain campaigns in Tyrol and Serbia. Transferred from Macedonia to the Western Front at the end of March 1916, the Alpenkorps had gone into general reserve before moving to Verdun, where, to the dissatisfaction of their commander, General Krafft von Dellmensingen, certain units were transferred to fill gaps in other divisions. At first their unusual appearance – from their Balkan campaigns they brought buffalo teams and painted wagons to the Western Front – made the Alpenkorps the butt of jokes, but they soon showed their fighting quality.

The village was only one of the obstacles that the Alpenkorps would have to face on 23 June. The little cluster of streets and houses was surrounded by a defensive system that included trenches, batteries, an important underground powder magazine and two fieldworks. The larger of these – known to the Germans from its shape as 'the Louse' – was situated on open slopes less than two kilometres beyond Fleury. From here it commanded Powder Magazine Ravine and Vine Ravine,

The main street of Fleury before 23 June 1916. *H P von Müller's estate*

two valleys that offered direct access to Verdun. The valleys also offered access to Belleville ridge, from where – if they got that far – the Germans would look straight down into the city. However, Belleville ridge was also the site of Forts Belleville and St. Michel, two older constructions that formed the last obstacles to the German advance. While the Germans did not regard them as capable of offering prolonged resistance, they were surrounded by a massive concentration of guns that had Fleury ridge in open sights. And with more guns on the flanks and on the Left Bank with similarly uninterrupted views, any Alpenkorps advance over the ridge was unlikely to be plain sailing.

The Alpenkorps front, which was little more than two kilometres long, lay in a sector bounded on the right by the ridge extending from Douaumont to Froideterre and on the left by Fontaine Ravine, a long valley running from the German-held village of Vaux to Fort Souville. On the right, the 1st Jägers were to maintain liaison with the Bavarian units attacking Thiaumont, before moving around Fleury village towards Fort Belleville. In the centre the Bavarian Leib Infantry – a Guard regiment – was to storm through the village and press on towards Belleville ridge, while on their left the 2nd Prussian Jägers pushed towards Fort St. Michel. For the first time, the front-line troops were to wear the new steel helmet, which weighed just over one kilogram and offered better protection than the old spiked helmet worn until then. While the new helmets were regarded as giving even the youngest recruit a look of reckless determination, acquiring one that fitted was no easy matter. Troops returning from the front gave up their

Above: German front-line troops of a Guards regiment wearing the new steel helmet. *Taylor Library*

Right: a rifleman of a Jäger battalion wearing his nountaineering rucksack. *Taylor Library*

helmets to men going forward and, as there was no time to try on different sizes, men took whichever helmet was available.

The French unit destined to meet the full force of the Alpenkorps assault was the 130th Division. Comprising the 39th, 239th, 405th and 407th Infantry Regiments, the division's left wing included *Abri 320*, an underground shelter for reserves close to Thiaumont, while, like the Alpenkorps, their right wing rested on Fontaine Ravine.

As darkness fell on 22 June, the assault companies of Jägers, infantry and pioneers, already tired by the long and hazardous journey from the camps to the north, crowded through Fort

Douaumont on their way to the front lines. It was an exhausting journey. The months of shelling had transformed the ground into a vast sea of craters through which the heavily laden troops had to pick their way. At midnight, with shells howling and screaming overhead – to the men listening it sounded as if all hell had broken loose – the commanders of the assault battalions moved out to their forward command posts and by 3am everyone was in place. The night was short and the troops who had been relieved had to use all speed over the broken ground to get through the fort and beyond before daybreak.

The Alpenkorps mustered eighteen battalions, with six in the front line, and by the time their tightly packed ranks moved off, the prolonged German bombardment had done its work. Hammered for two days by a devastating torrent of high explosive and gas that had obliterated their lines, cut communications and silenced the batteries in the central sector of the front, the French were dropping with exhaustion. However, they were quite clear about their orders – to fight to the last man – and as the attackers appeared through the smoke, they rose from their shell holes, caked with dirt and blood and brandishing their weapons like men possessed. It was in vain. Between *Abri 320* and Fleury two battalions of the 39th Infantry were completely submerged as the Leib Infantry, supported by specially trained storm

troops, roared down on them, wave upon wave, led 'as if on the parade ground' by their platoon leaders. Although French machine guns tore holes in their ranks, they reached the ruins of Fleury in little more than twenty minutes, surrounding and capturing the exhausted defenders of *Abri 320* on the way. In front of the village, two companies of the 239th Infantry scarcely had time to catch sight of the advancing waves before they too were submerged, their battalion commander being killed as he came out to face the Bavarians as they raced along the main street. In bitter fighting, the ruined houses and cellars were gradually cleared and by 9am Fleury was in Bavarian hands, apart from two stiffly defended houses on high ground at the south-eastern corner of the village. Here, a determined defence by a handful of men

Colonel Epp, commander of the Leib Infantry in Fort Douaumont. *H P von Müller's estate*

from the 239th Infantry caused the Bavarians substantial casualties and allowed reinforcements to arrive.

Having taken most of Fleury, Leib Infantry and pioneers fired off their last rockets and, receiving no response, pushed on towards Belleville ridge through their own artillery fire. The rockets were part of a complex system that had been devised to prevent misunderstandings between infantry and the artillery by marking the attainment of each planned objective. Fleury was to be attacked when white rockets from Thiaumont indicated the capture of a nearby road junction. The troops at Thiaumont would then wait for red rockets signalling that Fleury was in German hands before advancing further. However, in practice the system failed to work. The thunderous bombardment threw up such clouds of dust and smoke that the coloured rockets became indistinguishable and, to make matters worse, by 9am the French batteries on the Left Bank – which had not been gassed – were bringing down such a rain of fire between the advancing infantry and the rear that communication was cut off. With no means of knowing how far the troops had advanced, the artillery failed to lift its fire and this checked the momentum of the assault.

Despite the overwhelming force of the Alpenkorps attack, the French reacted vigorously. On their left, the gaping hole that the Bavarians had punched through the lines in Vine Ravine was rapidly blocked by reserves, who managed by superhuman effort to reach the ravine despite the gas. The French gas masks protected their wearers from phosgene better than the Germans had supposed they would, but they made breathing very difficult. Every step required a major effort and any shock that displaced the mask was likely to be fatal. Disconcerted by the sudden French riposte, the Bavarians were forced back in disorder as the reserves – a single battalion of Chasseurs and two infantry companies – deployed in a thin line across the 1,500-metre gap towards Fleury.

In the centre, the Leib Infantry's rapid progress towards Belleville ridge was caught in a rain of shrapnel from a French battery on the hillside below the village. French reserves coming up at speed towards Powder Magazine Ravine, where the roaring guns stood wheel to wheel, threw themselves forward, stupefied by the noise, to support the battery and prevent the Bavarians from reaching the vital valley. At the same time on the right, desperate French troops fought tooth and nail to prevent the Germans from reaching Fontaine Ravine. Without ammunition, food or water, cut off from the rear and suffering terrible casualties, they nevertheless managed to hold the attackers at bay and

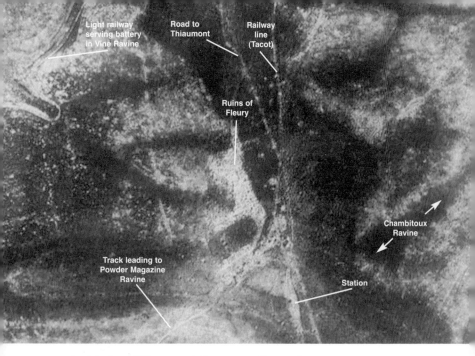

Aerial view of Fleury and the surrounding ravines. *H P von Müller's estate*

prevent them from reaching Fort Souville.

By midday the German advance had been checked. However, the French lines were not continuous, divisions and brigades had lost contact, and the position remained precarious. Throwing in all available reserves, General Nivelle, who had taken over from General Pétain as Second Army commander at the beginning of May, made an urgent appeal for reinforcements. In Verdun, the order was given for the immediate transfer of all services and supplies to the other side of the Meuse and steps were hurriedly taken to defend the city itself. During the afternoon the situation became sufficiently serious for General Pétain, who now commanded the Centre Group of Armies at Bar-le-Duc, to telephone General Headquarters with the message that, if the Germans reached Belleville ridge, it might become necessary to withdraw to the Left Bank. He emphasized that morale among the troops available for reinforcements was not high and asked for the Somme offensive to be brought forward.

By afternoon the effects of phosgene had worn off and French fire began to reach hurricane levels, preventing the arrival of fresh troops to relieve the exhausted assault units. This particularly affected the Alpenkorps, which had pushed further ahead than the units on either side and had taken heavy losses, particularly of officers. Messages received from German company commanders during the afternoon made it clear that any further advance was impossible. The men were at the end of their strength and, after a hot day, tormented by thirst, nothing more could be demanded of them without an immediate supply of water. If it were not forthcoming, serious reverses could be expected.

Across the front, the attacks were called off. On both sides exhausted men found what shelter they could, while the stretcher bearers went about their business and the endless bombardment continued.

Earlier that day, General Nivelle had issued an urgent appeal to the soldiers of the Army of Verdun from his headquarters at Souilly:

The hour is decisive ... Comrades, you will not let them pass.

They did not pass. In the German press the capture of Fleury and Thiaumont was hailed as a victory, but there had been no breakthrough. For a few hours the fate of the city had hung by a thread, but when night fell on 23 June, Verdun was still in French hands.

The walk

This walk begins at Fort Douaumont. To reach the start of the walk, take the D603 from Verdun towards Etain. (NB: on the IGN maps, this road is still numbered N3.) Follow the road uphill from Verdun and turn left at the junction with the D913

General Nivelle.
Taylor Library

following the sign to *Champ de Bataille 14–18*. When you reach the crossroads with the D112, where a wounded lion monument stands on the left, continue straight ahead to the next crossroads and turn right. With the military cemetery on your left, pass *Abri 320* and turn right on the D913d just before the Islamic Memorial, which looks like a small mosque. The junction is signposted *Fort de Douaumont*. Continue to the fort car park. The various defensive features to be seen before you reach the car park are described in Walk No. 8.

On 23 June 1916 Fort Douaumont was the headquarters of the Bavarian Leib Infantry. It was also the regimental first-aid post and

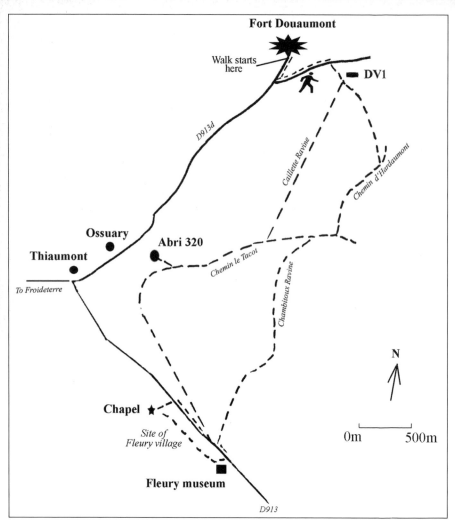

Fort Douaumont

Walk starts here

DV1

D913d

Caillette Ravine

Chemin d'Hardaumont

Ossuary

Abri 320

Thiaumont

Chemin le Tacot

Chambitoux Ravine

To Froideterre

N

Chapel

Site of Fleury village

Fleury museum

0m   500m

D913

collecting point for French prisoners of war taken in the Fleury sector. The rain of shells that had fallen on the fort since February had smashed the walls of the ditch, repeatedly blocked the entrances, and left the whole area a shapeless mass of interlocking shell craters. Inside, dirt and debris had piled up in the barrack rooms and corridors, which were packed with men, equipment and supplies. Difficult of access, heavily damaged and without water or sanitation, Fort Douaumont continued to offer food, shelter and a chance of rest to men returning from the front line or heading out towards its horrors in the direction you will now take.

From the car park, begin to walk back along the road. After a few metres, turn left on a wide grassy track signposted *Sentier de*

Infantry shelter DV1. *Author's collection*

Douaumont, Sentier d'Hardaumont. Pass the green and white barrier and continue for roughly 300 metres, then turn right downhill between forest blocks 365 and 359 following the sign for *Abri Infantrie DV1 100 mètres*. When you reach the ruined infantry shelter, stop. The design and purpose of these shelters is described in Walk No. 4. During the spring of 1916 this shelter, which is one of four between Fort Douaumont and Fort Vaux, was the scene of fourteen desperate German attacks that included flame throwers and even mining. It was finally captured at the beginning of April 1916 and remained in German hands until the French counter-offensive of October 1916.

Having inspected DV1, return to the wide grassy track that runs downhill between blocks 365 and 364. This begins within a few metres of the shelter. The skyline ahead is Fleury ridge, from where you would have been fully visible in 1916. The track crosses Caillette Ravine, an immensely important valley that formed one of the main supply routes between Fort Douaumont and Fleury during the Battle of Verdun. Continue for approximately one kilometre and turn right at the T-junction with a hard gravel track which on the IGN maps is named *Chemin le Tacot* (this is the bed of the old railway from Verdun to the Belgian border). The pine trees visible approximately 200 metres ahead mark the Bavarian front line of 23 June 1916. Pass the pine trees and continue along the Tacot track for roughly 500 metres, then turn right at the signpost reading *Sentier de Douaumont, Abri 320 200m, Fort de Douaumont 1580m*. Follow the path uphill to the first ventilation 'chimney' and stand with your back to the Ossuary. Fort Vaux is on the skyline to your left front, while Fort Souville is hidden in the high clump of trees on the skyline immediately opposite the 'chimney'. Even though these forts cannot be seen today, their commanding position – and the danger they posed to troops on this hillside – is perfectly clear.

Abri 320

This former underground shelter for reserves is similar to Four Chimneys Shelter (for a description, see Walk No. 5). On 23 June, *Abri 320* was just inside the French front line and was defended by the 39th Infantry. By the time the Bavarians arrived, prolonged shelling had ploughed the hillside into huge craters, smashed the trenches and blocked the entrances to the shelter, which had to be repeatedly dug out. The occupants were dropping with exhaustion and although they fought as best they could, they were soon overcome. Lieutenant Legris, whose grave is close to the information boards, was killed defending his machine gun post. He is commemorated in one of the memorial windows in the Ossuary chapel.

A view along the Tacot track. The Bavarian front line of 23 June 1916 crossed the Tacot from left to right just beyond the bend, where the track disappears from sight. *Author's collection*

Between 23 June and 24 October 1916, *Abri 320* functioned as a vital shelter, supply dump and command post for the German units in the Thiaumont-Fleury sector and was always overflowing with men. Sanitation was non-existent and conditions in the confined space underground were indescribable. In an attempt to improve them, German pioneers built tiers of bunk beds and divided the shelter into separate sections. They propped up the roof with pillars and beams and dug through the concrete on the Ossuary side in an attempt to make new entrances that were unknown to the dreaded French artillery. Suffocatingly hot, dark and streaming with condensation, the awful conditions inside were aggravated by a stink so overpowering that many troops were glad to leave, even though to do so meant facing the terrors of the front line.

Now return to the Tacot track and turn right. As you walk towards the junction with the D913, the pale rectangular building housing the memorial museum will come into view. It stands on the former site of Fleury railway station which, being on high ground overlooking the village, was bitterly disputed during the summer of 1916. The walk returns to the museum after visiting the destroyed village. Fort Souville stands in the high trees behind the museum.

Fleury

When you reach the D913, turn right along the road. The unending series of shell holes on the left-hand side are all that is left of the destroyed village of Fleury-devant-Douaumont, whose existence is commemorated in the roadside monument erected by the *Touring Club de France* after the war. When you reach the small roadside parking area, stop and face ahead.

You are standing on Fleury ridge, roughly halfway between the Thiaumont fieldwork and Fort Souville. In 1916 you would have been clearly visible from both Thiaumont, which is ahead of you, and Froideterre, which is to your left front. Now face downhill towards the small chapel. To your left, Fort Souville – which is out of sight through the trees beyond the museum – overlooks the hillside below you. Directly ahead of you, but invisible in the forest today, are Forts Belleville and St. Michel and a long railway embankment. In 1916 these three sites hosted a massive concentration of guns which had Fleury ridge in plain sight and, with the guns on the flanks, subjected the Bavarians to continuous, devastating fire.

In 1914 the little scattering of farms and houses that made up Fleury-devant-Douaumont formed the centre of an extensive fortified area. Being used to the presence of soldiers, the inhabitants went about their business as they had done for centuries, their lives governed by agriculture, the church, the climate and, latterly, by the little train that chugged up from the city. There were still a few civilians here in 1915 and although the houses were still standing when the Bavarian assault began on 23 June 1916, the intense bombardment soon ground them to powder. It was 11 July 1916 before the Bavarians gained control of the whole village and throughout the summer the French counter-attacked repeatedly, throwing men again and again into an unrecognizable landscape strewn with the debris and dead of earlier attacks. Having recaptured the site of the railway station, they continued to nibble away at the ruins until, on 18 August 1916, the famous Moroccan Colonial Infantry Regiment succeeded in regaining control of the hillside in front of you and pushing the Germans back beyond the D913. But by then Fleury had completely disappeared.

The site is a testament to the fury of those months. At the end of the war the French government ordered that the village should not be rebuilt and returning villagers were refused permission to stay. A chapel, a focus for Franco-German reconciliation, surmounted by the statue of Our Lady of Europe, was built on the site of the former

Fleury in ruins, October 1916.

Taylor Library

Memorial to the men of Fleury village who died in the First World War.

Author's collection

The memorial museum. *Author's collection*

church of St. Nicholas, but the rest of the village was gradually overtaken by forest until, by the late 1960s, it was invisible from the road. Clearance work carried out over the last thirty years has not only revealed the layout of streets and houses but also the unimaginable ferocity of the shelling. Like the other villages that died for France during the Battle of Verdun, Fleury has retained its legal existence. The war memorial, which stands on the site of the former *mairie*, or town hall, lists the men of Fleury who fell during the war and Mass is said in the chapel once a year. These, and the bits of stone and tile to be found by visitors hunting in the undergrowth, are all that remain to bear witness to life on the peaceful slopes above Verdun before the summer of 1916 swept it away for ever in apocalyptic combat.

From Fleury, return to the museum either by the D913 or by St. Nicholas Street, a former village street which is signposted close to the chapel. A visit to the museum may be convenient at this point.

Return to Fort Douaumont

To return to your car, cross the road in front of the museum and turn back towards Fleury. Just before you reach the fire warning sign (marked *Attention au feu*) look to your right across an open field. Fort Douaumont is on the skyline, little more than two kilometres away as the crow flies. Immediately beyond the fire sign, turn right on the dirt track that leads to a green and white barrier with a *Voie Privée* sign on the right. This marks the entrance to a forest road named the *Chemin des Chars*. Pass the barrier and follow the track downhill into Chambitoux Ravine, which – now the haunt of cuckoos – was one of the main German supply and access ravines for the Fleury front during the summer of 1916. As the track drops downhill, the French flag on the top of Fort Douaumont will come into view on the skyline, giving an idea of the commanding position of the fort in relation to the surrounding positions.

At the T-junction with the *Chemin le Tacot* (approximately 1,500 metres ahead), turn right and walk along the level track following *Sentier de Vaux*. Note the field grave of Jacques Louis Lyon, 119th Infantry, which is on the right just below the track. After approximately 100 metres, turn left at the sign reading *Abri d'Infanterie DV1* and *Batterie du Ravin de la Fausse-Côte*. Walk uphill, passing the grave of Paul Sommières, 75th Infantry, and after approximately 500 metres turn left at the sign reading *Abri Infanterie DV1 480m*.

The dense forest makes it impossible to grasp the importance of this area in 1916. During the Battle of Verdun this hillside dominated the old village of Vaux and commanded two ravines – Caillette Ravine on your left and Fausse Côte Ravine to your right – which offered access to Fort Douaumont. The French machine gun nests that packed this hillside blocked the German advance on Fort Vaux until the beginning of June 1916. It was known to both sides as a charnel house and shows intense shelling.

Continue past DV1 and at the T-junction approximately 250 metres further on, turn left. Continue to the D913d and Fort Douaumont.

Keeping a watch on the enemy. *Taylor Library*

Walk No. 7

FORT SOUVILLE

JULY 1916

Duration: three hours.

Distance: five to six kilometres.

This walk covers the final Alpenkorps assaults of 11 and 12 July 1916. It is covered by IGN maps 3112 ET and Blue Series 3212 Ouest. There is an uphill section of approximately one kilometre at the end of the walk but the rest is either level or downhill. It is likely to be muddy throughout the year. There is a picnic site at the back of the Verdun Memorial museum, which you will pass on the walk.

Warning: This route covers Fort Souville, the 155mm gun turret, the Powder Magazine and a number of other dangerous structures, which should not be entered. Walkers should also take care to avoid the remaining picket posts and wire when visiting the gun batteries at the rear of Fort Souville.

The events

At the end of the day on 23 June 1916 the centre of the German line on the Right Bank of the River Meuse formed a deep bulge which, lying in full view of the massive concentrations of guns around Fort Souville, Froideterre and the forts on Belleville ridge, was subject to constant, devastating fire. Plans were immediately drawn up for a further German offensive which would capture Fort Souville and thus remove part of the threat to the troops in the Fleury sector. It would also demonstrate that the Germans were not intending to abandon the fight. However, even while the plans were being prepared, General von Falkenhayn – knowing that the Allied offensive on the Somme was imminent – was ordering his commanders at Verdun to practise the most stringent economies in men, materiel and ammunition and withdrawing some reserve units and heavy batteries.

The new operation could not take place immediately, as further reserves of phosgene had first to be built up. It was therefore fixed for 8 July but before it could begin the weather turned wet. As phosgene needed dry weather to be effective, the operation was postponed until conditions improved. For days the rain poured down, collapsing the trenches and filling the shell holes – already a mass of corpses in all stages of decomposition – with foul, stinking mud. Soaked to the skin

Entrance to Fort Souville as seen after the battle. *Author's collection*

Entrance to former barracks of Fort Souville, 2008. *Author's collection*

and covered in mud, the exhausted Bavarian assault troops returned to their camps, their fighting capacity already diminished. It was some days before the weather changed and they could once again begin the long tramp through the constant curtain of shell fire to the unimaginable chaos of mud, rubble and interlocking craters that formed the 'front line' in the Fleury sector.

The offensive was to take place in two stages. First, the three divisions on the German left would seize a series of important positions close to Fort Vaux. At the same time, the battered Alpenkorps

– pressed into service once again – would clear Fleury station, push the remaining French defenders out of the village, and seize the crossroads in front of Fort Souville. This would bring the left of the line level with the centre and secure the approach to the fort. Then, while a specially trained battalion of Jägers stormed Fort Souville, the Leib Infantry would sweep downhill from Fleury, clear the French command posts on the hillside and seize an important underground ammunition store known as the Powder Magazine. If all went according to plan, Fort Souville and a number of other important positions would be in German hands by the end of the day.

On 10 July the German preliminary bombardment began. At the same time a number of reconnaissance patrols were sent out, during one of which a German officer was captured with orders for the following day. Realizing that a major assault was about to take place, the French poured such a roaring torrent of shells into the German lines that the earth seemed to boil. Conditions were particularly difficult for the Leib Infantry at Fleury who – in addition – suffered day and night from flanking fire from Froideterre Ridge. As casualties rose, men lost contact with one another and all order was lost. This made it impossible to organize the incoming units in coherent waves and they simply took up positions where they could, close together, in one or two lines.

Facing the Alpenkorps were a handful of under-strength units from the French 255 and 262 Brigades, with the 167th and 168th Infantry covering Fleury and the remnants of the 7th and 14th Infantry holding the approach to Fort Souville. In some places the front lines were less than 50 metres apart and on the high ground around Fleury station shelling had so totally destroyed all traces of organization that the defending troops had neither shelters nor trenches to help them. However, they did have new gas masks and when the phosgene bombardment finally began in the early hours of 11 July, it had no effect. Worse, the gas fired on Fort Souville settled downhill, particularly affecting the German units below the fort. Some of these had already suffered heavy casualties even before the offensive began. As a result of the relentless French bombardment they had arrived in position hopelessly disordered. They then made matters worse by bunching as far forward as possible, where – because the front lines were close together – the shelling was lightest. As companies and battalions became mixed up and officers lost contact with their men, some began to wonder whether the new operation was doomed even before it began. When it did, they had to attack up a steep hillside that

One of the sunken entrances to the Powder Magazine. *Author's collection*

was devastated by shelling and covered in a wild tangle of splintered tree trunks, roots, broken branches and wire. This made the advance so slow that the attackers presented an easy target and once again the operation ended with whole companies being wiped out. The situation was no better at Fleury station, where the attacking units met such a torrent of fire that anyone who tried to move forward was immediately mown down. As gaps appeared in the lines and officers fell, the survivors took cover in shell holes and the attack faltered. Seeing the units on either side of him unable to advance, the commander of the specially trained fortress assault battalion realized that any attempt on Fort Souville was hopeless. Unwilling to cause needless bloodshed, he took the bold step of ordering that the attack on the fort should not take place.

For the Bavarian commanders crowded together in Fort Douaumont the sound of uninterrupted French artillery fire signalled that the phosgene bombardment had been ineffective. However, with rocket signals invisible in the smoke, all they could do was to wait for messengers to reach the fort with definite news. It was almost five hours before a message arrived with news of success: the Leib Infantry's attack on the Powder Magazine – a former underground ammunition depot – had been successful.

At jump off, some Leib units had cleared the remaining houses in Fleury while others had moved swiftly down the hillside. Capturing an important complex of dugouts housing the French battalion command posts for the Fleury sector, they continued to the Powder Magazine, attacking the entrances with machine guns and flame throwers. The Germans' own bombardment was still falling on the Powder Magazine when the first Bavarians arrived, but they pushed boldly through it and scrambled down into the deep cut that led to the western entrance. Quickly setting up a machine gun, they opened fire on the iron grille that barred the entrance, at the same time as another group armed with flame throwers poured the flames and smoke into the eastern entrance. The tunnels, which were situated just above the bottom of the ravine, were already full of gas and they now filled with suffocating black smoke. For the occupants, who had already suffered a colossal twenty-four-hour bombardment with the heaviest calibre shells, which had sent terrifying shock waves through the magazine, this was the last straw. Within a short time a white cloth was poked through the grille and, haggard, filthy and smoke blackened, the defenders emerged. They included many wounded and gassed, as the magazine had served as a dressing station for the front line. Altogether at least 250 men, including staff officers, stretcher bearers, medical personnel and priests, were taken prisoner and sent back towards Fort Douaumont. Exploring inside, the Germans found large stores of ammunition and other supplies including, to their delight, tinned meat, biscuit and chocolate.

While this was happening, other Bavarians were pressing home the assault in different directions. With shells falling all round them, some men pushed along the hillside from the Powder Magazine towards a fieldwork officially named the *Ouvrage du Bois Fleury*, but known to

Battlefield debris. The oval water bottles at the front of the photo are German. *Author's collection*

the Bavarians – from its shape – as the Louse. This fieldwork was important, as it dominated the two ravines through which the French could supply the Fleury front. It was also in direct communication with Souville, St. Michel and Belleville, the three forts directly threatened by the day's offensive. Unnoticed in the chaos, the Bavarians reached the Louse and stormed it, taking the defenders by surprise and marching them back to German lines. At the same time another little group managed to reach the main road from Verdun to Fleury (the D112), crossed it and continued uphill, arriving at the top of the ridge close to Fort Souville. There were no French in view but no Germans either and – despite glimpsing the River Meuse and part of the city – the little group turned back.

In the middle of the day a lull in the shelling allowed both sides to organize their positions. Despite some success on the German left wing, the new line was not an improvement on the old one. While Fleury village was now entirely in Bavarian hands, the area around the station remained obstinately French, blocking progress towards Fort Souville. Furthermore, the Leib Infantry's new line was merely a series of shell holes that lay in full view of Forts Souville and St. Michel, and their losses, particularly of officers, had been very severe. Reinforcements were needed and with them came orders for a second attempt to take Fort Souville.

By now the fort was a ruin and conditions inside were chaotic. The devastating pounding it had received during the battle had filled the ditch with earth and rubble, torn up the surrounding wire and smashed the stonework but, even damaged, it remained a vital front-line observatory and its underground shelters offered accommodation for staffs, reserves, signallers and medical personnel. The little garrison was commanded by Lieutenant Colonel Astruc de Saint-Germain, a retired cavalry officer aged 65 who had served in the Franco-Prussian war of 1870. During the morning, a handful of survivors from a company of the 7th Infantry, who had been sent up to reinforce the French front line in the Souville sector, had arrived at the fort to find the commander gassed and most of the garrison out of action. With violent shelling preventing them from reaching their positions, the company commander, Lieutenant Kléber Dupuy, decided to remain in the fort and organize the defence. Rounding up a lieutenant to keep order inside, he posted sentries, set up the available machine guns and took command.

At dawn on 12 July the Bavarians attacked again. Capturing the minute handful of defenders still desperately clinging to the ruins of

German dead collected for burial. *Taylor Library*

Fleury station, they reached the crossroads in front of Fort Souville with unexpected speed. However, as the attackers pressed forwards, they were caught in a terrible French artillery barrage and, unable to withdraw, a small group was driven on towards the fort. As soon as they appeared, Dupuy led his men out. Violently attacked, leaderless and unsupported, the little group was unable to resist, but they had been seen by observers at Fort Douaumont and triumphant reports were sent back that Fort Souville was at last in German hands. It was some hours before the true position became clear and, when it did, all hopes of a German breakthrough at Verdun finally died.

By the time this attempt on Fort Souville took place, General von Falkenhayn had ordered the Fifth Army to go on the defensive. He now withdrew a large number of batteries to meet the offensive on the Somme. Although the French may not have known it at the time, they could at last begin to breathe more easily.

The walk

This walk begins at the memorial museum (*Mémorial de Verdun*). To reach the start of the walk, take the D603 from Verdun towards Etain. (NB: on the IGN maps, this road is still numbered N3.) Follow the road uphill from Verdun and turn left at the junction with the D913, which

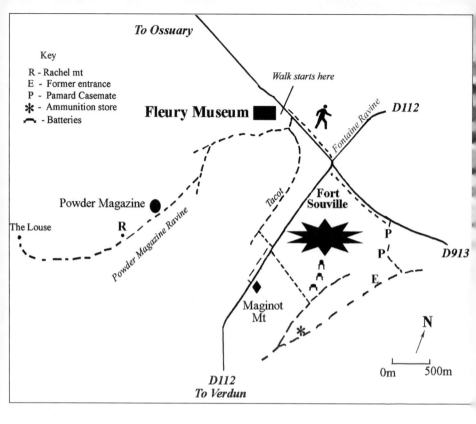

To Ossuary

Key

R - Rachel mt
E - Former entrance
P - Pamard Casemate
✱ - Ammunition store
⌒ - Batteries

Fleury Museum ■

Walk starts here

D112

Fontaine Ravine

Powder Magazine ●

Fort Souville

Tacot

The Louse

R

Powder Magazine Ravine

P

P

D913

E

Maginot Mt ◆

✱

N

0m   500m

D112
To Verdun

is signposted *Champ de Bataille 1914–1918.* At the crossroads with the D112, where a wounded lion monument stands on the left, drive straight ahead and park by the memorial museum, which is the square building a short distance ahead on the left. Having parked, walk back to the lion monument, then stop and look back the way you have come.

The area between this crossroads and the museum (formerly Fleury station) was one of the most bitterly contested on the whole Verdun battlefield. Ploughed by thousands of shells, it was a landscape without hope in which men lived, fought and tried to survive amid smashed guns, dead horses, rotting wood, rusty iron, piles of ammunition, personal equipment, corpses and rats. The crossroads, which commands the approach to Fort Souville and the Fleury sector from both the German and French sides, was captured by the Germans on 12 July and recaptured by the French in a dawn assault seven days later. By then the chapel of Sainte Fine, which is marked by the small memorial standing across the road from the lion, had been reduced to a pile of rubble. It has never been rebuilt.

The wounded lion marks the official high-water mark of the German offensive, although small groups did manage to get slightly closer to the city. The French divisions listed on the side are those that fought in the Battle of Verdun, while the four infantry regiments recorded at the end under the lion's head are those that met the full force of the headlong Alpenkorps assault on 23 June.

Fort Souville and Pamard Casemate

Fort Souville – described by General Pétain as the last bolt on the door to Verdun – stands in the trees some 300 metres behind the lion. One of the first forts to be built at Verdun after the French defeat in 1870, Souville was originally built of stone and protected by the traditional ditch and drawbridge, but it was later modernized by the addition of strong underground shelters and a retractable gun turret. The fort's commanding position – from its highest point the views stretched for miles in all directions – made it vital to the defence of Verdun, and it became even more important once Forts Douaumont and Vaux had fallen into German hands. When that happened, the garrison was strengthened, water reserves were increased and all non-essential troops were ordered out.

During the desperate summer of 1916 this old fort was of the utmost importance to the French and throughout the months of roaring bombardment it continued to offer shelter, rest, command and medical facilities to troops in the front line. After the battle it was estimated that the Germans had used between 9 and 10 million francs' worth of

The wounded lion, which marks the official high-water mark of the German advance. *Author's collection*

ammunition to achieve 1 million francs' worth of damage. Although the parts above ground were largely destroyed, the underground shelters remained habitable. Construction and repair work carried out in 1917 and 1918 included the excavation of a well, a tunnel system and three machine gun turrets of a type known as Pamard Casemates. **All parts of Fort Souville are extremely dangerous today and visitors should not attempt to enter any of them.**

From the lion monument walk uphill along the D913 following the sign reading *Fort de Vaux*. After approximately 400 metres you will reach a parking area on the right. Turn right here towards *Casemates Pamard modèle 1917*.

The Pamard Casemates at Fort Souville were intended to cover dead ground and to provide close defence in the immediate surroundings of the fort. Named after their French inventor, Commandant Pamard, who saw service at Fort Genicourt to the south of Verdun, they were cheaper and quicker to install than the rotating machine gun turrets on Fort Douaumont. They were also more reliable, as the rotating turrets often became jammed by debris thrown into the works during shelling. The thick armour plating – which looks faintly like an elephant's trunk – protected two machine guns which were mounted side by side and fired alternately to avoid overheating. Some Pamards had shuttered apertures in the roof for use with an observation periscope. Forts Douaumont and Vaux were clearly visible from here during the Battle of Verdun.

Now take the gravel path that runs to the left of the casemate. Pass the second Pamard Casemate and follow the path, which runs downhill to a T-junction with a dirt road, crossing a substantial communication

One of the Pamard Casemates at Fort Souville. *Author's collection*

trench as it does so. At the T-junction, turn right along the *Sentier de Souville* and walk on until you reach a sign reading *Entrée de Guerre*. This points towards the entrance to the former barracks of Fort Souville from where tunnels, now collapsed, offered protected access into the main body of the fort. Continue along the track, noting the picket posts and wire emerging from the ground along the left-hand side and also the deep communication trench, part of the extensive network of trenches which were in constant use during the battle. Continue along the level track for approximately 400 metres, passing the entrance to one of the underground ammunition depots that served this sector. At the T-junction a short distance ahead, turn right. As you walk uphill, note the collapsed dugout entrances lining the bank on the left. A little further on you will see the earthworks of a pre-war 155mm gun battery. The battery and ammunition niches are described on the information plinth by the path. Pass the battery and at the sign reading *Depôt de munitions, Tourelle de 155m. 150m., Casemate Pamard*, continue to the 155mm gun turret, which is the low building directly ahead. Note the heavy shelling on either side of the footpath and the communication trench that runs up to the gun turret.

The 155mm gun turret

This revolving turret for two short-barrelled 155mm guns is unique. When first designed in the early 1870s it was to be raised and lowered by steam power. At the time, manufacturing techniques were not sufficiently advanced to produce it, and it was not until the late 1880s that this modified version was built. Even so, the design proved problematical and the difficulties were not finally resolved until the end of 1915. Although the guns saw action at the beginning of the Battle of Verdun, an explosion in one of the barrels soon damaged the turret mechanism. This was only repaired in March 1917, when the boiler, which was slow, complicated and smoky, was replaced by a 12hp electric engine. Subsequently the turret, which was now only equipped with a single gun, was linked by tunnels to Fort Souville, the underground shelters and an emergency exit.

Once the guns were out of action, this turret served as a front-line command post. The unsuccessful French operation to retake Fort Douaumont was commanded from here in May 1916 and on 11–12 July it formed the headquarters of 262 Brigade, which took the brunt of the German assault between Fleury and Fontaine Ravine.

Walk to the top of the turret to view the massive steel cupola that covers the gun, then follow the path towards the other defensive

The 155mm gun turret at Fort Souville in 1916. *Taylor Library*
The 155mm gun turret in 2007. *Author's collection*

features on this ridge. These include the armoured observation post installed in 1917, another Pamard Casemate and a damaged shelter which forms part of the pre-war gun battery you saw earlier. In 1916 the views from here stretched for miles in all directions, although there was often so much smoke and dust in the air that it was impossible to see even as far as the Memorial museum. It is unfortunate that these views, which are so important to an understanding of the Battle of Verdun, are today blocked by trees on all sides.

Maginot monument and Powder Magazine

From the Pamard Casemate follow the beaten path towards the ammunition niches you saw earlier. When you reach the sign reading *Depôt de munitions* etc., turn right on a wide dirt track and follow it downhill to the D112, then turn left and walk along the road. The first two monuments to be seen on the left commemorate Lieutenant Kléber

128

Dupuy's last-ditch defence of Fort Souville on 12 July 1916 and the site of the command post used by General Chrétien, commander of XXX Corps, at the start of the Battle of Verdun. A short distance further on stands the monument to André Maginot, a member of the French parliament and government minister, who gave his name to the Maginot Line of sunken forts constructed along the eastern border of France between the two world wars. It represents the wounded Maginot being carried on a rifle from the site of the ambush into which his group fell on 9 November 1914 (see Walk No. 2).

From the Maginot monument, retrace your steps along the road. At the sign reading *Massif Fortifié de Souville*, turn steeply downhill on an unmarked grassy track. At the T-junction with the former light railway embankment (*Chemin le Tacot*), turn right. Walk ahead for approximately 750 metres to the T-junction with the *Sentier de la Poudrière*, which is marked by a red circle. Turn left downhill. Pass the sign reading *Ravin de la Poudrière* and continue downhill to a fork in the path. Take the right-hand fork between blocks 561 and 579 and follow the red circles until you reach the sign reading *Vestiges de la Poudrière*. This points to the eastern entrance of the magazine. The western entrance, which was the first to be attacked by the Bavarians, is some 50 metres further on. Powder Magazine Ravine, one of the two vital supply and access valleys to the Fleury front, is behind you as you face the entrance.

This major ammunition depot was constructed before the First World War to supply neighbouring gun batteries and the smaller depots in the area. It was shaped like a letter H, with two parallel tunnels

The monument to André Maginot, who gave his name to the Maginot Line of forts. *Author's collection*

linked by a third tunnel running at right angles between them. Various side chambers offered storage space for ammunition and supplies, and the tunnel entrances – which were served by a light railway – were closed by a steel door and an iron grille. Throughout the Battle of Verdun the magazine functioned as a command post and centre of resistance and offered shelter, rest and medical facilities to French units in the area. It was recaptured by the French in a night attack on 19 July.

The heavily damaged building to the right of the entrance is all that remains of the guard house, in which the commander of 255 Brigade, Lieutenant Colonel Coquelin de Lisle, set up his headquarters for the defence of Fleury. The monstrous bombardment of 10 July cut communications by telephone, blinker lamp or pigeon and left the

French machine gunners operating a captured German Maxim 08.
Taylor Library

The guard house of the Powder Magazine. *Author's collection*

brigade staff dependent for information on runners or passing infantrymen. Alerted on 11 July that a strong force of Bavarians was nearing the magazine, Coquelin de Lisle ordered all important papers to be burnt and, rounding up his staff, left the guard house. He was killed before he had gone 50 metres. Coquelin de Lisle is commemorated on a plaque in the Fleury section of the Ossuary.

Rachel monument, return to Fleury

The walk now returns to Fleury Memorial. If you wish to see the impressive memorial to Corporal André Rachel before you return, continue along the Poudrière path for some 300 metres before returning here. Corporal Rachel, a machine gunner with the 167th Infantry, was killed on 11 July 1916 as the Bavarians swept along the hillside. Most of the gun crew died with him.

To return to Fleury from the magazine, retrace your steps uphill and when you reach the level track (*Chemin de la Poudrière*) turn right. A short distance beyond the junction of tracks the collapsed entrances to a number of dugouts can be seen on the left. These formed the command posts of two of the French front-line battalions defending the Fleury sector on 11 July 1916. Although stiffly defended, the Leib Infantry managed to capture the two battalion commanders; this, together with the death of the brigade commander, Coquelin de Lisle, left the French command structure in the area seriously disabled.

From here, continue uphill to the Memorial to return to your car.

Fort Souville. *Taylor Library*

Walk No. 8
THE FRENCH COUNTER-OFFENSIVE
24 OCTOBER 1916

Duration: two and a half hours.
Distance: four kilometres.

This walk covers the actions of the 4th Mixed Regiment of Zouaves and Tirailleurs and the Moroccan Colonial Infantry during the French counter-offensive of 24 October 1916. It is covered by IGN maps 3112 ET and Blue Series 3212 Ouest. The forest path between Douaumont village and the fort is likely to be muddy throughout the year.

The route cannot be walked on Mondays and Tuesdays, when the firing range close to Fort Douaumont is in operation.

The events

The fact that on 11 July 1916 General von Falkenhayn had ordered the Fifth Army to adopt a defensive attitude did not mean that fighting stopped at Verdun. Both sides were determined to give the impression that further offensives were still possible and each wished to prevent the other from withdrawing troops and equipment for use on the Somme. Over the next few weeks the French launched numerous desperate and costly counter-attacks on German lines, little by little retaking such vital positions as the Sainte Fine crossroads and the Powder Magazine, and finally clearing the site of Fleury village in August. Faced with a degenerating situation at Verdun and believing that the resources expended there could be better used elsewhere, the German High Command made a number of top-level changes. On 23 August, General Schmidt von Knobelsdorf, the Chief of Staff of the Fifth Army, who favoured continuing the offensive,

Field Marshal von Hindenburg. *Taylor Library*

was replaced by the less hawkish General von Luttwitz. This was followed a few days later by the replacement of the Chief of the German General Staff, General von Falkenhayn, by Field Marshal von Hindenburg. Visiting Verdun with General Ludendorff on 2 September, Hindenburg declared it to be a running sore and ordered the immediate cessation of all attacks.

At the same time, however, the French High Command began to prepare for a major operation on the Right Bank that would liberate Forts Douaumont and Vaux and push the German line away from Verdun. The first task was to increase railway capacity, establish secure telephone links with the front lines and repair the roads. On the battlefield, communication trenches were deepened, supply and ammunition dumps prepared, and command posts, dressing stations and shelters constructed. It was a monumental task. After so many months of shelling the battlefield was a scene of horror, with a stench so appalling that the troops put garlic in their nostrils to keep it out. To make matters worse, it rained for weeks. The newly dug positions collapsed and, as the

trenches filled with water, a tacit truce came into being. Despite the weather, the task of preparing for the offensive was pushed on with all speed. At the beginning of October work began on the jump-off trenches, and a number of high-ranking visitors – including Field Marshal Sir John French – came to inspect the work. Behind the lines, French troops trained intensively in the new tactics learned during the Battle of Verdun. These involved mixed assault units of machine gunners, pioneers and lightly armed, fast-moving infantry.

On 20 October the rain stopped and the French guns roared into action. For four days an avalanche of gas and fire poured into the German lines, forcing the defenders to wear their masks for hours at a time. Trenches, shelters, batteries and observation posts were hurled into the air; camps and reserve positions were pounded and giant shells from two huge 400mm howitzers rocked Fort Douaumont and Fort Vaux. The German batteries returned fire as best they could but a shortage of ammunition made it impossible to offer any effective defence and, with gun barrels worn, many of their shells fell short. German front-line units soon became cut off from one another and in the Douaumont sector, where the exhausted 54th Division held the

French troops parading ready to move up. *Taylor Library*

lines, it was only by crawling on all fours that messengers could reach the fort.

The French operation on the Right Bank was to be led by three divisions, with the 38th facing Fort Douaumont. Some weeks earlier, the 38th had gone into training at Stainville near Bar-le-Duc, where the selected area had been carefully laid out with every physical obstacle represented, including a full-scale outline of Fort Douaumont. Each day the troops methodically rehearsed the operation, envisaged every possible difficulty and planned how to overcome it. During the first half of October officers and section leaders were taken to Verdun, where they carefully reconnoitred the ground, visiting their starting positions and the communication trenches leading to them. On 21 October the Division arrived at Verdun and spent the night at the Citadel. The next day the men drew the necessary ammunition, equipment and rations and went into position on the battlefield in rear of their start line, where, for the next two nights, they were all employed in repairing the trenches destroyed by rain and enemy artillery, which caused numerous casualties.

Zero hour was 11.40am on 24 October. The task of retaking the vital

General Charles Mangin, commander of the French offensive of 24 October 1916.

Taylor Library

positions between the Thiaumont fieldwork and Fort Douaumont had fallen to the Moroccan Brigade, which was composed of two extremely distinguished regiments: the Moroccan Colonial Infantry (MCI) and the 4th Mixed Regiment of Zouaves and Tirailleurs. Zouaves and Tirailleurs were light infantry raised in France's North African possessions, but while the Tirailleurs were native troops, the Zouaves were Frenchmen.

The plan was for the 4th Mixed to take the ruined fieldwork before moving ahead along the ridge to Douaumont village. This would secure the left flank of the MCI, whose objective was Fort Douaumont. At 11.39am on 24 October the Tirailleurs battalion jumped off in thick fog with the Zouave battalion 150 metres behind. They were accompanied by machine gunners, flame thrower units and a company of Senegalese, whose task was to mop up the captured trenches. After weeks of rain the sector was a scene of total desolation, with water-filled shell holes stretching in all directions. Despite the state of the ground the leading battalion made good speed. Quickly reaching the remains of Thiaumont, they overcame the exhausted defenders, who were up to their knees in mud and water and completely cut off. Leaving a small group to hold the position, they pressed on over the devastated battlefield with light artillery units

PC 119, command post of the 4th Mixed on 24 October 1916.

Author's collection

knocking out any strongpoints that still remained active. In three-quarters of an hour the Tirailleurs reached the first objective, where they dug in. They were soon passed by the Zouave battalion, which swept on to Douaumont village and linked up with the MCI at Fort Douaumont.

The task of retaking Fort Douaumont had been entrusted to the Moroccan Colonial Infantry, the most highly decorated regiment in the French army. An exclusively French formation, the MCI was raised originally from troops on service in Morocco, to which Senegalese or Somali units might be attached in exceptional circumstances. The plan was for the 4th Battalion to seize the enemy's front lines and dig in halfway to Fort Douaumont. The 1st Battalion would then move forward to encircle the fort, while the 8th, supported by flame-thrower units, cleared the fort and held it. At 11.40am the 4th Battalion jumped off from positions just below the Thiaumont fieldwork but met unexpected resistance and only reached the first objective at 1pm. Shortly afterwards the 1st Battalion moved past them, believing the 8th to be close behind. However, when they reached Fort Douaumont the assault battalion was nowhere to be seen. Not wishing to give the Germans time to react, the leading waves of the 1st surged into the ditch and onto the superstructure. A few minutes later the 8th Battalion came up, having been delayed by a compass error. They immediately went into action with automatic rifles, grenades and flame throwers to clear the fort.

By now Fort Douaumont was in a terrible state. On 23 October several huge 400mm howitzer shells had bored through the concrete roof of the fort, filling the corridors with smoke and fumes, hurling men against the walls, smashing the roof of the main corridor and blowing the infirmary into rubble. In addition, a roaring fire had started in the main pioneer depot and in the accompanying explosion the commandant was knocked unconscious. The pioneer depot was situated next to a huge store of hand grenades and – fearing a repeat of the massive explosion of May 1916 – the acting commandant ordered evacuation. However, in the confusion the order did not reach everyone and some men remained behind. They worked desperately to put out the fire, but by evening almost everyone was gassed and runners sent out with messages failed to return. Believing that it was impossible to hold Fort Douaumont any longer, the senior officer in the fort, Captain Soltau, ordered the final evacuation. As dawn was breaking on 24 October 1916 the last of the German garrison left Fort Douaumont.

But even as they were leaving another small group was returning.

Infantry shelter MF 2, near Froideterre, the command post of 38th Division for the offensive of 24 October 1916. *Author's collection*

Assessing the damage, they found that the fire in the pioneer depot had burned down and that the gas had dissipated. The roof was smashed in several places and the main corridor was blocked by debris, but communication from one side of the fort to the other was still possible by the lower floor. The commander of the returning group – the fort's former artillery officer, Captain Prollius – ordered the remaining machine guns to be set up to defend the entrances and sent out urgent messages for reinforcements and supplies. No answer was received and, knowing that the French assault was imminent, Prollius called his officers together. Each man was asked for his opinion and all agreed that they had no choice but to surrender. Hurriedly destroying maps and papers, the little group of twenty-eight officers and men gathered together in one of the barrack rooms, the last garrison of the once mighty fort. When the first two French soldiers entered the barracks a lieutenant went towards them with hands raised, sadly surrendering Fort Douaumont after eight months of German occupation.

The walk

This walk begins at the Ossuary. It is mostly a road walk, as the relevant forest paths are too muddy and overgrown to be practicable. To reach the start of the walk take the D603 from Verdun towards

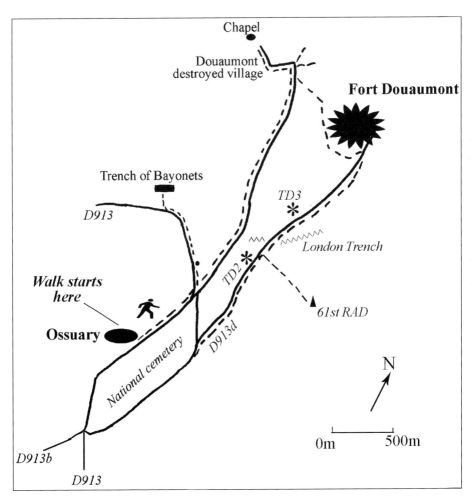

Etain. (NB: on the IGN maps, this road is still numbered N3.) Follow the road uphill from Verdun and turn left at the junction with the D913 following the sign reading *Champ de Bataille 1914–1918*. At the crossroads with the D112, where a wounded lion monument stands on the left, drive straight ahead, following *Ossuaire*. At the next crossroads you will see the military cemetery and Ossuary ahead of you. Drive uphill and park, then walk along the road at the front of the Ossuary with the cemetery on your right. At the junction with the D913, turn left and follow the road past the *Abri des Pélerins* café and downhill to the entrance to the Trench of Bayonets (*Tranchée des Baïonnettes*). The tree-covered hill to be seen on the distant skyline ahead when you reach the entrance to the Trench is the Mort-Homme, which was clearly visible from here in 1916.

Now face the entrance. The valley behind you is Dame Ravine, a

Part of a ruined infantry entrenchment at the top of Dame Ravine.
Author's collection

steep-sided and winding valley which offered sheltered access between the Meuse valley to your left rear and the important ridge to your right. It was commanded by a number of infantry entrenchments that were strategically placed around the head of the ravine. Access to the ravine from the hillside in front of you was blocked by an extensive trench system known to the Germans as 'the Honeycomb'. Dame Ravine had to be taken if the Germans were to continue their movement along the ridge to your right, and during June 1916 fighting here reached levels of unparalleled intensity. Although the far end of the ravine (to your left) was in German hands by 8 June, this end was only finally captured on 23 June 1916. It was known to both sides – with good reason – as Death Ravine.

The Trench of Bayonets memorial was built on the initiative of an American citizen, Mr G F Rand. It commemorates an event that took place between 11 and 13 June 1916, when units of the 137th Infantry were holding the Honeycomb against Bavarian regiments, who were trying push down into Dame Ravine. Throughout May the strongly defended Honeycomb – German records speak of 'countless machine guns' – successfully repulsed all assaults, and when the Bavarians took over the sector they were determined to deal with it once and for all. On 8 June, an assault by two regiments was defeated by desperate French resistance. A second assault carried out the following day also came to nothing, and further attempts were called off until the artillery had done its work. For three days the Honeycomb was subject to a hurricane of shells, and on 12 June the Bavarians attacked again. By then, the French defenders were dropping with exhaustion. Some of the forward companies had been reduced to ten men, streams of blood ran everywhere and the ground was covered with every form of human debris. Surrounded and subjected to concentrated machine gun fire, the French fought off repeated assaults until, without ammunition, food, water or hope of relief, the tiny handful of survivors was forced to surrender.

In January 1919, the commander of the 137th, visiting the sectors where his regiment had fought, found rifles emerging from the earth on this hillside. The story quickly spread that the rifles – there was no mention of bayonets at the time – belonged to an entire unit that had been buried alive by shelling as the men prepared to attack. A small memorial was put up, a copy of which is to be seen above the right-hand side of the paved pathway. The present huge memorial was built in 1920. No bayonets are to be seen today. The original rifles were stolen long ago and the current replicas are firmly cemented into the ground against thieves. Although the popular story differs from the accounts of survivors of the event, the Trench of Bayonets may be regarded as a monument to the many men on both sides who were buried alive by the constant, thunderous bombardment that characterized the Battle of Verdun.

The original monument on the site of the Trench of Bayonets. Note the absence of vegetation. *Author's collection*

Douaumont village during the Battle of Verdun. *H P von Müller's estate*

From the Trench of Bayonets, return to the top of the hill. At the crossroads a short distance beyond the café, turn left at the sign reading *Douaumont village détruit* and walk along to the site of the destroyed village of Douaumont.

Like the other villages that were swept away by the Battle of Verdun, Douaumont has never been rebuilt. The short white posts on either side of the pathways indicate the site of each house and give the name and occupation of the inhabitants in 1914. A plan of the village and fort is to be seen at the junction of the two streets. Once each year Mass is said in the chapel, which stands on the site of the former village church. On 2 March 1916, Captain Charles de Gaulle, commander of 10th Company, 33rd Infantry, and future President of France, was wounded in the German attack on this village. Taken prisoner, he was treated in hospital in Maintz before being interned in a camp in Osnabrück for the rest of the war.

After visiting the village, return to the road and take the path to be seen at the edge of the trees on the other side of the road. This is signposted *Fort de Douaumont 800 mètres*. When you enter the forest you are on the glacis of Fort Douaumont, which is now a mass of tangled vegetation through which the path winds through deep water-filled shell holes. The path passes close to the ditch, which has recently been cleared of trees, leaving the great earth rampart and one of the machine gun turrets clearly visible. This approach gives an indication of the original strength of Fort Douaumont and the dangers of approaching it over the open glacis in 1916.

On reaching the car park of the fort, turn right and follow the D913d back towards the Ossuary. The recently restored graves of two unknown French soldiers are to be seen a short distance beyond the car park on the left. A little further on, a footpath to the right signposted *Stèles Basques 40 mètres* leads through an area of spectacularly deep shell holes to the graves of three casualties of the unsuccessful French attempt to retake Fort Douaumont in May 1916. As you continue

One of the many thousands. *Taylor Library*

towards the Ossuary you will pass several interesting features including, on the right, the ruins of infantry shelters TD3 (*Abri 2408*) and TD2 (*Abri Adalbert*), which are almost as damaged as the Thiaumont fieldwork. In 1916, batteries flanked the combat shelters but no trace of them can to be seen today and the ground inside the wood is a mass of shell holes. A plan to link *Abri 2408* with the Bourges Casemate at Fort Douaumont, drawn up in 1917, was never implemented. On the left is a well-excavated section of the *Boyau de Londres*, a strong communication trench that connected Belleville Ridge to Fort Douaumont via Froideterre and *Abri 320*. The present appearance of the trench dates from refurbishment carried out in 1917. A short distance beyond the *Boyau de Londres*, a sign on the left reading *61ième RAD 400 mètres* points to a memorial to five members of a field artillery regiment who were killed by shelling in July 1917 while digging shelters in an adjacent ravine. If you wish to visit this monument, be warned that it is a steep pull back up to the road. The walk ends at the Ossuary.

The London Trench. *Author's collection*

Walk No. 9
THE CENTRAL BATTLEFIELD MONUMENTS
Duration: one hour.
Distance: one and a half kilometres.

This walk begins at the Ossuary and covers the main monuments in the centre of the battlefield. It is covered by IGN maps 3112 ET and Blue Series 3212 Ouest. To reach the start of the walk, take the D603 from Verdun towards Etain. (NB: on the IGN maps, this road is still numbered N3.) Follow the road uphill from Verdun and turn left at the junction with the D913, following the sign to *Champ de Bataille 14–18*. At the crossroads with the D112, where a wounded lion monument stands on the left, drive straight ahead following signs to *Ossuaire*. At the next crossroads, you will see the military cemetery and Ossuary ahead of you. Drive uphill past the Jewish memorial, then park and walk to the main entrance. Stand with your back to the doorway and face ahead.

Introduction

In the summer of 1916 all you would have seen from here was unimaginable desolation. The months of shelling had churned the ground into a sea of shell holes that were strewn with every sort of debris. As the endless bombardment meant that the dead could not be buried, this area was – in the words of one French colonel – 'paved with corpses'. All movement took place at night and by day men cowered in whatever shelter they could find, hoping to survive. This was the ground that the Germans had to cross as the lines were pushed

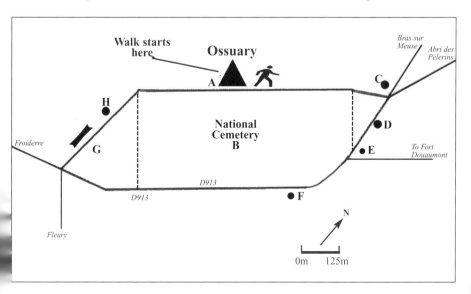

slowly from Fort Douaumont to Fleury, an advance of less than three kilometres as the crow flies but a journey of pure horror through a constant, terrifying curtain of fire. During the French counter-offensive of 24 October 1916, this same devastated wilderness was crossed by the Moroccan Colonial Infantry in three hours of slow and exhausting advance from their starting line – a short way beyond the Jewish memorial to your right – to Fort Douaumont, whose shattered outline was almost invisible among the mountains of earth flung up by the shells.

Since 1918 nature has reclaimed the battlefield, which is mostly hidden in dense forest. However, certain sites have been cleared: the nine destroyed villages and this hillside, whose serene monuments now commemorate the devastation and loss of life suffered by both sides during the terrible months of 1916.

The Ossuary (A)

The Ossuary owes its origin to the work of Monsignor Ginisty, Bishop of Verdun from 1914 to 1946, who travelled the world to raise money

Wounded French infantry awaiting evacuation to the rear. *Taylor Library*

The Ossuary. *Author's collection*

to build a final resting place for the men whose bones scattered the battlefield. Contributions were obtained throughout the world from cities and states whose coats of arms can be seen above the windows along the front of the building. The first stone was laid in August 1920 but it was 1932 before the Ossuary was formally inaugurated. It is said to represent the hilt of a sword that has been thrust into the ground against the invader, although the central tower also bears a strong resemblance to an artillery shell. It houses the remains of some 130,000 men, whose bones are visible through the small windows along the wall at the rear of the building.

Inside, the long central gallery features forty-six stone 'coffins' set in alcoves. Each alcove commemorates a particular sector of the battlefield and any human remains found in that sector are placed in the corresponding vault on the lower floor. The engraved plaques on the walls and ceiling commemorate individual soldiers or units that served at Verdun. They include many brothers, such as Augustin and André Recapet, 74th Infantry, who were killed on consecutive days during the first French attempt to retake Fort Douaumont in May 1916. Their names are recorded on a stone to the left of the monumental *poilu* close to the main entrance. Among the thousands of French names are two 'English' ones: Arthur Exshaw and Samuel Chew. Exshaw, whose name appears on the right-hand wall of the La Caillette alcove close to the entrance to the tower, was a member of an Anglo-Irish family that had settled in the Cognac area of south-western France. While some of his relatives served in the British Army, Arthur joined the French 49th Infantry and was killed in the first attempt to retake Fort Douaumont in May 1916. Samuel Chew was a volunteer with the American Field Ambulance Service. He died on service in

Bone collection after the war *Taylor Library*.

1917 and his name appears in the Avocourt alcove, which is next to the Malancourt section. To the left of that section, a plaque commemorating the loss of Emile Imhaus de Mahy and his four sons would make any visitor's blood run cold.

The chapel's memorial windows were dedicated by individual families to their fallen sons. They include, in the second window on the left, Jean Legris (or Legrix), who was killed in the fighting for *Abri 320* on 23 June 1916 (see Walk No. 6). The window nearest the altar on the right-hand side commemorates a number of named nurses, although women only served in the Verdun sector after 1917. The embroidered chasuble in the glass case on the steps was saved from a

Looking from the site of the Ossuary to Fort Douaumont, which is on skyline in the centre of the picture. Note the absence of vegetation. The handwritten inscription reads 'Souvenir of June 1920'. *Author's collection*

89. THIAUMONT — L'Ossuaire, au fond le fort de Douaumont — The Ossuary

burning church by an American soldier, Frank Havlik, in 1918. He wore it under his uniform and believed that it brought him safely home at the end of the war. It was recently presented to the Ossuary by his grandchildren.

The great tower, which was paid for by American donations, includes a small museum with relics of the destroyed villages, stereoscopic views of the battlefield and a collection of weapons. Although there are over two hundred steps, it is worth a climb on a clear day as the views are astonishing. At certain times of the year a revolving lantern at the top of the tower lights the battlefield at night – an unforgettable sight made disturbing by a pane of red glass in the lantern that gives the impression of a red eye sweeping over the devastated landscape.

The national cemetery (B)

The cemetery in front of the Ossuary contains the bodies of 15,000 men who were brought here for reburial, a section at the northern end being dedicated to Muslim soldiers who died for France. The bronze plaque between the two flights of steps records the first joint visit to Verdun of the leaders of France and Germany in 1984, at which the two countries were formally reconciled. The French regiments represented in the cemetery are listed on the wall below the plaque. General Anselin, who is buried in front of the wall, was killed at his command post close to Fleury shortly before the start of the French counter-offensive on 24 October 1916.

The 44th Territorials (C)

After visiting the cemetery, return to the road in front of the Ossuary. Turn right and walk towards the junction with the D913, keeping the Ossuary on your left. On the left of the junction is a small monument to the 44th Territorials, a local French regiment known affectionately as the 'terrible torials'. This was the regiment that André Maginot joined in August 1914 (see Walk No. 2).

The Islamic memorial (D)

Now turn downhill towards the Islamic memorial, which looks like a small mosque. This new addition to the monuments commemorates all the Muslim soldiers who died for France during the First World War. It was inaugurated by President Chirac of France in June 2006. Its construction required extensive forest and ground clearance, and during January 2006 visits to this area were severely restricted while ammunition disposal was in progress. The state of the ground to the left of the building provides dramatic evidence of the effects of shelling here during 1916.

Soldat du Droit (E)

From the Islamic memorial continue downhill to the junction with the D193d and turn right. The statue by the roadside of a recumbent figure wearing French uniform represents Second Lieutenant André Thomé, known as the *Soldat du Droit*. Thomé, who was a member of the French parliament, was mobilized in the dragoons but seconded at his own request to the infantry. He was killed on the Mort-Homme on 10 March 1916, aged 36.

Abri 320 (F)

Continue ahead with the Ossuary on your right until you reach a path on the left that leads to *Abri 320*. For a description of this type of underground shelter for reserves, see the section on Four Chimneys Shelter in Walk No. 5. The fighting that took place here in June 1916 is described in Walk No. 6. The shell-torn aspect of the ground between the two 'chimneys' gives an idea of the state of this entire area at the end of the Battle of Verdun. The difficulty of crossing such ground at any time but particularly when heavily laden, in wet and slippery conditions or at night, can easily be imagined.

The Jewish memorial (G)

Return to the road, turn left and walk to the next road junction, keeping the cemetery on your right. At the junction, turn right uphill. The

Memorial to the 44th Territorials. *Author's collection*

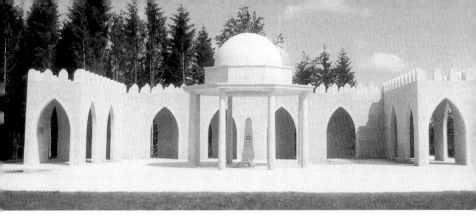

The Islamic memorial. *Author's collection*

substantial memorial on the left approximately 200 metres further on commemorates Jewish soldiers of France and allied nations and foreign volunteers who died for France during the First World War. Its design recalls the Western Wall of the Temple, and the two tablets are inscribed with the beginning of each of the Ten Commandments. It was erected in 1938 and remained undamaged during the Second World War.

Monument to the 4th Régiment Mixte (H)

The small monument to the right of the Jewish memorial commemorates the fighting for the Thiaumont fieldwork during the summer of 1916 and its recapture by the 4th Mixed Regiment of Zouaves and Tirailleurs on 24 October of that year (see Walk No. 8). The plaque at the back refers to Pierre Teilhard de Chardin, who served as a front-line stretcher bearer with this regiment.

The Soldat du Droit. *Author's collection*

The Jewish memorial. *Author's collection*

As you continue to the car park, note the small monument on the left to Jean de Lattre de Tassigny, who fought in this sector in 1916 and went on to high command in France and Indochina during and after the Second World War.

The ground over which the 4th Mixed Regiment attacked on 24 October 1916. *Author's collection*

Walk No. 10
A TOUR OF VERDUN CITY CENTRE

Duration: two hours.
Distance: roughly four kilometres.

This walk takes in a number of places in the centre of Verdun that have First World War connections. It does not cover every possible site of interest nor provide an overall history of the city. The route is covered by the street map named *Verdun: plan de ville*, which is produced by Blay-Foldex and on sale at the bookshop in Verdun's main shopping street (Rue Mazel).

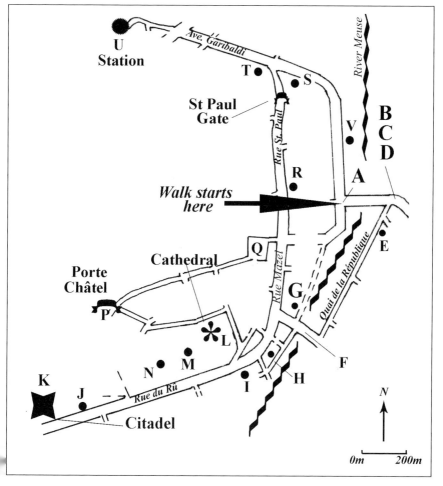

The Porte Chaussée. *Author's collection*

The walk begins in the centre of Verdun by the Porte Chaussée gate
(A). This is the fourteenth-century city gate with twin towers that
stands at the end of the bridge over the River Meuse. There is a paying
car park close to the gate, by the police station.

With the city gate behind you, walk across the bridge to the war
memorial, which stands on the left **(B)**. This memorial, which is built
on part of the old city ramparts, commemorates the men of Verdun
who fell during the First World War and military and civilian victims
of the Second World War. It was inaugurated in 1928. From left to right
the five soldiers represent a cavalryman, a pioneer, an infantryman
wearing the new uniform and steel helmet introduced in 1915, an
infantryman wearing the 1914 uniform, and an officer, also wearing
the 1915 uniform. They stand with their backs to the wall, symbolizing
the 'human rampart' that stopped the German offensive in 1916. A
plaque on the wall to the right of the memorial commemorates the
colourful military career of General Charles Mangin **(C)**, who planned
the French counter-offensive of October 1916, in which Fort
Douaumont was retaken from the Germans. The statue on the plinth by
the roundabout to your right rear **(D)** represents General Sarrail,
commander of the French Third Army, who was responsible for the

defence of Verdun during the first two years of the war.

Now face the river. The massive building programme undertaken at Verdun in the wake of the defeat of France in 1870 involved, in addition to forts, the construction of many barracks and other military buildings. This required a substantial labour force, which, together with the rapidly growing military population, made Verdun a very prosperous place. In 1916, shells fired from German naval guns some twenty kilometres to the north caused substantial damage here, particularly along the river bank to your right front. Reconstruction plans soon ran into problems, as they involved taking over former military areas. It was only in 1926 that the French government agreed to the changes and work could begin. It included demolishing certain sections of the seventeenth-century city walls and opening up the area to your left.

From the war memorial, cross the road and begin to walk towards the next bridge, keeping the river on your right. The handsome stone and brick building immediately beyond the *Canal du Puty* – which is part of the defensive system designed in the seventeenth century by Louis XIV's celebrated military engineer, Vauban – is the former Officers' Mess **(E)**. It was undamaged during the Battle of Verdun and remained in use until recently. Looking across the river from the Officers' Mess you will see the impressive Victory monument, which features a cloaked and helmeted warrior. This is dealt with in the later part of the walk.

Verdun city war memorial. *Author's collection*

Continue to the next bridge **(F)** (*Pont Legay*) and cross to the other side of the river, then stop and face ahead. On your right is the *Quai de Londres* and on your left is the *Quai Général Leclerc*. To your right front, a large white plaque on the wall of a building close to the corner with the *Quai de Londres* records the adoption of Verdun by the City and County of London in December 1920 **(G)**. In 1916 the *Quai de Londres* was the site of multi-storey houses and shops, whose lowest floors were at water level. During 1916 and 1917, shells aimed – unsuccessfully – at the two bridges you have just crossed caused serious damage here and the buildings were demolished after the war. The quay's present appearance dates from the major refurbishment of the city centre undertaken a few years ago.

Now cross over to the *Quai Général Leclerc* and walk ahead with the river on your left. The building with the handsome colonnaded front to be seen on the right halfway along this quay is the theatre **(H)**, which was opened in 1893 and played an important part in the cultural life of Verdun before the First World War. It is still furnished in the grand style, with glorious tiers of red and gold boxes and a ceiling full of cherubs.

At the corner beyond the theatre, turn right into the *Rue Victor Schleiter*. Continue to the next corner, then turn left into the *Rue Victor Hugo* and walk ahead. The substantial building with tall arched windows now on your left **(I)** is the recently restored market hall. Continue along the street with, first, the market hall and, second, a public car park, on your left. Beyond the car park the street narrows and the name changes to the *Rue du Rû*. Note the cathedral, Bishop's Palace and upper Citadel towering above you on the hilltop to the right. During the Napoleonic Wars, the upper Citadel served as a major prison for captured Royal Navy officers. When you reach the next road junction – a small roundabout with a bridge on the left – keep straight on along the *Avenue du 5ème R.A.P.* following signs to the *Citadelle Souterraine (Underground Citadel)*, whose massive walls will now be in view. The long building to be seen on the right approximately 100 metres beyond the roundabout – part of which has two floors – is all

A general view of the city of Verdun after the war. *Taylor Library*

The former military pigeon loft. *Author's collection*

that remains of the former military pigeon loft (**J**). The small square windows in the upper floor were originally the entrance hatches used by the pigeons. It was to this building that Fort Vaux's last carrier pigeon, the aptly named Valiant, returned on 4 June 1916, dying soon after its arrival. The bird was awarded a citation and a ring in the colours of the Legion of Honour before being stuffed and mounted for exhibition (See Walk No. 4).

The Citadel (**K**) was originally the central defensive stronghold of this city. Designed by Vauban and constructed in the late seventeenth century, the original redoubt was greatly extended in the late nineteenth century by the excavation of several kilometres of wide underground tunnels. Further tunnels were dug shortly before the outbreak of war. Safe under 16 metres of rock, the tunnels were not affected by shelling, and during the Battle of Verdun the Underground Citadel, with its flour mill, huge bakery, steam heating and electric ventilation, became a logistic and supply centre of enormous importance and offered shelter and accommodation to large numbers

The Faubourg Pavé military cemetery, where the other 'Unknown Soldiers' are buried. *Author's collection*

of troops, staff officers and municipal services. Most of the regiments that took part in the Battle of Verdun passed through it. To visit the tunnels, continue to the flagpoles and turn right through the door marked *Manutention*. The visit includes, among other things, scenes from life in the tunnels during the battle, a 'virtual flight' over the Lorraine countryside and a description of the selection of the Unknown Soldier, who was chosen here from eight unidentified French soldiers taken from different sectors of the Western Front.

The selection of one soldier to represent all those who died for France during the First World War was made on 10 November 1920 by Auguste Thin, a young war veteran serving with the 132nd Infantry. The selected coffin was transported to Paris and subsequently interred beneath the Arc de Triomphe, while the remaining seven were buried in Verdun. They surround the central cross in the Faubourg Pavé military cemetery on the *Avenue du Maréchal Joffre*. The cemetery is easily recognized by the six field guns that stand close to the entrance.

After visiting the Citadel, return to the road and turn left along the *Avenue du 5ème R.A.P.* At the roundabout, retrace your steps along the *Rue du Rû.* The old square building with side buttresses to be seen on the right immediately after the roundabout is a former church, which was used as a military stable during the war. Continue to the market hall, where the road forks. Take the left fork into the *Rue Gros Degrés* and, at the junction with the *Rue du Pont des Augustins*, turn sharp left up a steep flight of steps. At the top of the steps, continue ahead towards the *Ecole des Garcons*, then turn left towards the cathedral **(L)** (*Place Monsignor Ginisty*). As you walk up to the main entrance, which is opposite the *Rue de la Cathédrale*, note the shell damage along the wall on the left.

First founded around AD 450, the cathedral of Notre-Dame – one of the first churches in France to be dedicated to the Virgin Mary – has been extended and rebuilt many times. Although not seriously damaged during 1916, the cathedral suffered greatly during the bombardments of April and May 1917, which brought down the roof of the nave, damaged some of the side chapels and much of the cloister but left the towers largely untouched. Restoration, which was only completed in 1935, brought to light a number of features which had been destroyed or blocked up in earlier times. These include the crypt under the High Altar, where the capitals of the central columns are decorated with First World War scenes, including trenches, French and German soldiers and artillery.

War damage in Verdun. The Rue des Gros Degrés is on the left of the picture. The single-storey building on the right is the market hall. Just beyond it, the building with the high, ornamented roof is the theatre.
Tom Gudmestad

A wartime view of damage to the Bishop's Palace. *Tom Gudmestad*

After visiting the cathedral, turn left out of the main door and walk through the second archway into the courtyard of the former Bishop's Palace (*Palais Episcopal*) **(M)**, which was seriously damaged during the war. Now restored, the buildings house, at the upper end of the courtyard, the World Peace Centre **(N)** (*Centre Mondial de la Paix*) and, at the lower end, the Bishop's Library, which has an important collection of First World War books and documents. On the long metal plaque set at ground level in front of the entrance to the Peace Centre, snatches of letters by French and German soldiers are intermingled. Covering every subject from the weather to farming, food and their hopes of return, their words are a poignant memorial to the identical thoughts and sufferings of the men on each side of the battle.

Now return through the archway to *Place Monsignor Ginisty* and turn left uphill into the *Place Châtel*. At the top end of the Place, follow the *Rue Porte Châtel*, which is on the right, to the twelfth-century Châtel gate **(P)**. Pass through the gate and turn right into the *Rue Mautroté*, noting the grey water tower which was a gift from the City and County of London. Follow the *Rue Mautroté* downhill, passing two crossroads, and continue straight ahead into the *Place de la Libération*, where you will see the Victory monument **(Q)**.

This imposing monument, which was inaugurated in June 1929 in the presence of great crowds, comprises a monumental pillar on which stands a cloaked and helmeted warrior who is thrusting his sword into the ground against the invader. It is flanked by two Russian guns, which were captured by the Germans on the Eastern Front and then

German troops parading in front of the Victory monument on 16 June 1940.
H P von Müller's estate

recaptured by the French. The crypt inside the pillar is open to visitors. It contains a list of recipients of the Verdun Medal and the first volume of the *Livre d'Or*, which records the name of every French soldier who fought at Verdun. The inscription to the left of the door quotes General Pétain's famous Order of the Day of 10 April 1916: *Courage – we'll get them!*

From the Victory monument, go down the steps to the *Rue Mazel* and turn left. Continue for a short distance to the junction with the *Rue St. Pierre* and stop. The church of St. Nicholas **(R)**, which is on the right of the junction, still shows considerable shell damage on either side of the entrance doors. Immediately beyond the church, the Collège Buvignier, with yellow and green tiling, was a distribution centre for the French and American Red Cross. After the war, American generosity provided comfort to returning refugees at various places in and around Verdun, including a canteen at the station, a dispensary and a milk distribution centre.

Pass the junction and continue along the street, which is now named the *Rue St. Paul*. At the *Hôtel de la Cloche d'Or*, on the right, Ernest Jünger, the celebrated author of *Storm of Steel*, spent several days in 1913 before joining the Foreign Legion. His service did not last long, as he was under age at the time he signed up. During the Battle of Verdun, the buildings opposite this hotel, which now house administrative offices and the Court, were used as a hospital. Continue towards the double-arched gate which stands in the middle of the road ahead. During 1916, the substantial building to the right of the gate with *Hôtel Vauban* over the door **(S)** was used by American ambulance drivers. From this building, which also functioned as a triage and hospital, ambulances left on the dangerous journey to the first-aid post at Bras-sur-Meuse, some six kilometres to the north. The ambulances were housed in the St. Paul barracks which, now demolished, stood to the left of the town gate. In 1932, the Hôtel Vauban was one of the hotels used by the American Gold Star Mothers Pilgrimage. This was a United States government programme that offered the mothers or widows of members of the American Expeditionary Forces the possibility of travelling to the grave sites with all expenses paid.

Pass the St. Paul gate – a former town gate that still retains the chains and machinery used in former times to operate the drawbridge – and continue to the next road junction, then turn left into the *Avenue Garibaldi*. The monument in the grassy area on the left **(T)** commemorates Victor Schleiter, member of parliament for the Meuse Department and post-war mayor of Verdun, who was responsible for

The St. Paul gate. *Author's collection*

the reconstruction of the city. Continue towards the railway station, which is the pinkish-brown building directly ahead of you at the end of the street. When you cross the road junction (*Rond-Point des Etats-Unis*), note the monument to two vital military supply routes, the *Voie Sacrée* of 1916 and the *Voie de la Liberté* of 1944, each of which served Verdun. Continue into the station yard.

Externally, the present building **(U)** is a close copy of the original. It was designed by the famous Gustave Eiffel, who also designed the Eiffel Tower in Paris. Between 1914 and 1916, Verdun railway station served as a hospital and evacuation centre for thousands of wounded and, although it was damaged during the Battle of Verdun, it was not put out of action. The plaque to the right of the main entrance records the departure to Paris of the train bearing the Unknown Soldier on 10 November 1920. Opposite the station, the old Hotel Terminus, now a bar, accommodated pilgrims to the battlefield after the war was over.

From the station, return along the *Avenue Garibaldi*. When you reach the junction by the St. Paul gate, continue straight ahead with the gate on your right. Follow the road as it bends to the right along the

A wartime postcard showing French and American troops in front of Verdun railway station. *Tom Gudmestad*

river bank and continue towards the Porte Chaussée. As you do so, you will pass the mighty Rodin sculpture entitled *The Call to Arms*, which

was presented to Verdun after the war by the people of Holland **(V)**. The sculpture represents a raging Fury, who is protecting an exhausted warrior while arousing France to one last great effort. Rodin had originally submitted the design to a competition for a monument to commemorate the defence of Paris in 1871 but it was rejected as too startling and the model lay neglected for years. It was only after Rodin's death that a committee in Holland raised money to have it cast to commemorate the victorious defence of Verdun.

The walk ends at the Porte Chaussée gate.

Select Bibliography

French sources

Les armées françaises dans la Grande Guerre, Service Historique, Ministère de la Guerre, Tome IV: Verdun et la Somme, Vols. 1, 2 and 3 (Paris, Imprimerie Nationale, 1926)

Verdun et ses forts pendant la guerre, General G Benoît, 1929 (Archives du Mémorial de Verdun)

Le drame du fort de Vaux, Colonel Raynal (Frémont, Verdun, Les Editions Lorraines, [1935])

Verdun 1916, Jacques Péricard (Nouvelle Librairie de France, 1947)

Verdun, Fleury-devant-Douaumont, Juillet 1916, General Michel (1st published 1966; repr. Comité Nationale du Souvenir de Verdun, Mémorial de Verdun)

Verdun, Jacques-Henri Lefebvre (Paris, Editions du Mémorial, [1996])

Regimental histories too numerous to list individually.

German sources

Der Weltkrieg 1914–1918, Vol. 10: Die Operationen des Jahres 1916; Vol. 11: Die Kriegführung im Herbst 1916 und im Winter 1916/17 (Reichsarchiv/Kriegsministerium, Berlin, E S Mittler & Sohn, 1938)

Schlachten des Weltkrieges, Vol. 1: *Douaumont*, Werner Beumelburg

—— Vol. 13: *Die Tragödie von Verdun 1916*: Part I: *Die deutsche Offensivschlacht*, Ludwig Gold

—— Vol. 14: *Die Tragödie von Verdun 1916*, Part II: *Das Ringen um Fort Vaux*, Alexander Schwencke

—— Vol. 15: *Die Tragödie von Verdun 1916*, Part III: *Toter Mann–Höhe 304*; Part IV: *Thiaumont–Fleury*, Ludwig Gold (Oldenburg/Berlin, Verlag Gerhard Stalling, 1925, 1926, 1928 and 1929)

Die Höhe Toter Mann, Markus Klauer (Velbert, Gesellschaft für Druck und Veredelung, 2001; ISBN 3-9807648-0-X; available at outlets in Verdun and from the author)

Die Höhe 304, Markus Klauer (Velbert, Gesellschaft für Druck und Veredelung, 2002; ISBN 3-9807648-1-8; available as above)

Regimental histories too numerous to list individually.

On the city of Verdun

Verdun à la veille de la guerre, Edmond Pionnier (1st published 1917;

Verdun, Les Editions Lorraines, 1994)

Verdun: ville Militaire, L. Frémont, L. Rodier, P. Gauny, J.-P. Harbulot, G. Domange and A. Bernède (Verdun, Collection Connaissance de la Meuse, 2000)

Verdun ruins. *Taylor Library*

Further Reading

The following are suggested in addition to those listed in the Select Bibliography.

In English

Verdun

Education before Verdun, Arnold Zweig (New York, Viking, 1936)
The Price of Glory, Alistair Horne (London, Macmillan & Co. Ltd., 1962)
Verdun, Georges Blond (London, André Deutsch, 1965)
Fort Douaumont: Verdun, Christina Holstein (Battleground Europe series; Barnsley, Pen & Sword Books, 2002)
The Road to Verdun, Ian Ousby (London, Jonathan Cape, 2002)
German Strategy and the Path to Verdun, Robert T Foley (Cambridge University Press, 2005)

General background

My War Experiences, Crown Prince William of Germany (London, Hurst & Blackett, 1922)
Paths of Glory: the French Army 1914–1918, Anthony Clayton (London, Cassel Military, 2003)

In French

La Bataille de Verdun, Maréchal Pétain (Paris, Payot, 1929)
Douaumont 24 Octobre 1916, Gaston Gras (Frémont, Verdun, Les Editions Lorraines, [1934])
Combattre à Verdun, vie et souffrance quotidiennes du soldat 1916–1917, Gérard Canini (Presses Universitaires de Nancy, 1988)
Verdun: les forts de la victoire, Guy Le Hallé (Paris, Citédis, 1998)
Douaumont: 25 février–25 octobre 1916, Werner Beumelburg, translated by Lieutenant Colonel L Koeltz (Paris, Payot). Long out of print, this is a French translation of the fascinating Douaumont volume of *Schlachten des Weltkrieges* referred to in the Select Bibliography.

In German

Verdun 1916, Hermann Wendt (Berlin, E S Mittler, 1931)
Verdun: das Grosse Gericht, P C Ettighoffer (Gütersloh, Bertelsmann, 1936)
Verdun: Souville, Hermann Thimmermann (Munich, Verlag Knorr & Hirth GmbH, 1936)
Verdun: die Schlacht und der Mythos, German Werth (Augsburg, Weltbild Verlag, 1990)

Battlefield Guidebooks

There are few English-language guides to the Battle of Verdun. The Michelin Guide, *Verdun and the Battles for its Possession*, first produced in 1919, is interesting but has little detail. It was reprinted in 1994 by G H Smith & Sons, Easingwold, Yorkshire, England. A useful general guide to the battlefield is *A Historical Tour of Verdun* by Jean-Pascal Soudagne and Remi Villagi. This is published by Editions Ouest-France in three languages and is on sale in Verdun and on the battlefield. Verdun and the wider area are covered by Major and Mrs Holt's guide to *The Western Front: South*, published by Pen & Sword Books, UK, 2005. The fighting for Fort Douaumont, detailed tours of the fort and a driving tour of the surrounding area are contained in my book *Fort Douaumont: Verdun* in Pen & Sword's Battleground Europe series (2002). There is also a section on Verdun in Rose Coombs' *Before Endeavours Fade*. For anyone who reads German, I recommend *Spurensuche bei Verdun: ein Führer über die Schlachtfelder* (Bonn, Bernard & Graefe Verlag, 2000), by Kurt Fischer and Stephan Klink. This offers a short history of the battle and guides visitors through both major and lesser known sites, lists German cemeteries in the area, and includes a section on well-known Germans – such as Hermann Göring – who were present at Verdun during 1916.

The banks of the Meuse, and the Cathedral. *Taylor Library*

Short Glossary

Glacis – A cleared area of sloping ground outside the ditch of a fort, which could be swept by fire from the ramparts.

Infantry entrenchment – A substantial rifle pit of stone or concrete, often with metal shields to shelter the troops. They were of considerable length and could accommodate large numbers of defenders.

Bourges Casemate – A strong concrete bunker armed with two quick-firing 75mm fortress guns. These were installed in two chambers placed slightly one behind the other and shielded from direct fire by a long wall. The embrasures allowed for fire in one direction only. The name comes from the experimental range at Bourges, France, on which they were first tested.

Chasseurs and **Jägers** – French and German light infantry.

Zouaves – Light infantry recruited from Frenchmen in France's North African possessions.

Tirailleurs – Light infantry recruited from the native population in France's overseas possessions.

Pioneers – Specialist troops with various skills including field fortification. Those referred to in this book were trained in infantry tactics and advanced with the leading waves, clearing away wire and other obstacles.

75mm gun – A French 3-inch calibre, quick-firing artillery piece.

155mm gun – A 6-inch calibre artillery piece.

Useful Addresses

The Verdun tourist offices may be contacted in English.

Maison de Tourisme, Address: Place de la Nation, BP 60232, 55106 Verdun Cedex.
> Tel. + 33 3 29 86 14 18, fax + 33 3 29 84 22 42
> Email: verduntourisme@wanadoo.fr
> www.verdun-tourisme.com

Office de Tourisme, Address: Pavillon Japiot, Ave. Général Mangin, 55100 Verdun
> Tel. + 33 3 29 84 55 55, fax + 33 3 29 83 44 23
> Email : tourisme@cc-verdun.fr

Battlefield sites

Please note that opening times may change without warning. At the time of writing visiting times are as follows:

Fort Douaumont
Outside: any time.
Inside: 1 February–31 March and 1 October–30 December from 10 till 1 and 2 till 5.
1 April–30 June and 1 September–30 September from 10 till 6.
1 July–31 August from 10 till 7.
Closed mid-December to end of January.

Fort Vaux
Outside: any time.
Inside: 1 February–31 March and 1 October–19 December from 9.30 till 12 and 2 till 5.
1 April–30 June and 1 September–30 September from 9 till 6.
1 July–31 August from 9 till 6.30.
Closed mid-December to end of January.

Mémorial de Verdun (Fleury Memorial museum)
Address: 1, Ave. du Corps Européen, 55100 Fleury-devant-Douaumont
Tel. + 33 3 29 84 35 34, fax + 33 3 29 84 45 54
http://www.memorial-de-verdun.fr/
Spring and summer from 9 till 6.
Autumn and winter from 9 till 12 and 2 till 6.
Closed mid-December to mid-January.

The Ossuary
Address: 55100 Douaumont
Tel. + 33 3 29 84 54 81, fax + 33 3 29 86 56 54
http://www.verdun-douaumont.com
January: closed; February: open in the afternoon; then April to
August from 9 till 6 (weekends) and 10 till 6 (weekdays).

Monument de la Victoire
Place de la Libération, Verdun.
The crypt is open daily from approximately 9.30 till 11.30 and from
2 till 6. Entrance is free.

Centre Mondial de la Paix (World Peace Centre)
Address: BP 183, 55105 Verdun Cedex
http://www.centremondialpaix.asso.fr/
Tel. + 33 3 29 86 55 00, fax + 33 3 29 86 15 14
The World Peace Centre, which is situated in the former Bishop's
Palace next to the Cathedral, houses permanent and temporary
exhibitions on the theme of war and peace, liberty and human rights.
Open daily from 9.30 till 12 and 2 till 6.

Citadelle Souterraine
Open December, February and March: 10 till 12 and 2 till 5
April to June and September: 9 till 6, July–August: 9 till 7
October to November: 9.30 till 12.30 and 2.30 till 5.30.
Closed in January.

To visit the **Kaiser Tunnel** (a German supply tunnel in the Argonne
Forest) contact:
Office de Tourisme du Pays d'Argonne,
Address: 6, Place de la République, 55120 Clermont-en-Argonne,
France
Tel. + 33 3 29 88 42 22, fax + 33 3 29 88 42 43
Email: tourisme.argonne@wanadoo.fr

To visit the **Moro Lager/Camp Moreau** (a restored German
camp), contact:
Maison du Pays d'Argonne
Address: Rue St. Jacques, 51800 Vienne le Château, France
Tel. + 33 3 26 60 49 40
Email: mpa@argonne.fr

Butte de Vauquois

A wonderfully preserved site, which was the scene of intense mine warfare. The craters may be visited at any time but to visit the museum and the underground installations contact:

Les Amis de Vauquois et de sa Région
Address: 1 rue d'Orléans, 55270 Vauquois, France
http://pagesperso-
    orange.fr/vauquois.guerre.14.18/acceuil_english.htm

French troops receive decorations after the fighting at Verdun. *Taylor Library*

Acknowledgements

In writing this book I have been greatly helped by the generosity of friends who gave their time, expertise and resources to help me. The responsibility for any errors or omissions in the finished work is mine alone. My thanks go first to Isabelle Remy and Antoine Rodriguez of the Mémorial de Verdun for maps, books and other resources and to the staff of Fort Douaumont and Fort Vaux for their many kindnesses. Two of my children, Isabella and Valdemar, accompanied me on the early walks, leaving me with shining memories of the empty battlefield in winter and spring. Geoff Mangin and Burleigh Randolph read much of the text and drew attention to numerous points that were unclear. Markus Klauer and Tom Gudmestad kindly supplied photos from their personal collections, while Jan Carel Broek Roelofs provided much information and generously allowed access to the wonderful photographic archive of the late H P von Müller. My thanks are also due to the Beumelburg family of New Zealand and Germany for the photo of the young Werner Beumelburg, whose account of the fighting for Fort Douaumont is such a masterpiece. Finally, Tony Noyes, who came to Verdun long before I did, offered his unrivalled knowledge of the Western Front, Verdun and the German Army and accompanied my many trips to the battlefield. He read the text as I wrote it, suggested routes, helped with maps and was always ready with a glass of wine at the end of the day. I could not have written it without him. Tony, this book is for you.

Luxembourg,
June 2008

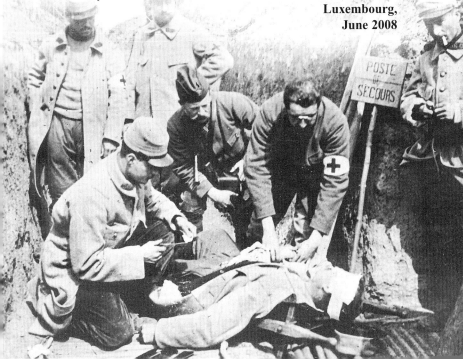

INDEX